RAISING MUSICAL KIDS

Raising Musical Kids

◆ ◆ ◆

Great Ideas to Help Your Child
Develop a Love for Music

Patrick Kavanaugh

Servant Publications
Ann Arbor, Michigan

Vine Books is an imprint of Servant Publications especially
designed to serve evangelical Christians.

Scripture references are taken from the Holy Bible, *New
International Version.* © 1973, 1978, 1984 International Bible
Society. Used by permission of Zondervan Bible Publishers.

Published by Servant Publications
P.O. Box 8617
Ann Arbor, Michigan 48107

Cover illustration: Young Girls at the Piano by Pierre-Auguste
Renoir. The Metropolitan Museum of Art, Robert Lehman
Collection, 1975. (1975.1.201) © 1989 by The Metropolitan
Museum of Art.
Back cover photo: Allen Thornburgh
Cover design: Multnomah Graphics.

95 96 97 98 99 10 9 8 7 6 5 4 3 2 1

Printed in the United States of America
ISBN 0-89283-903-1

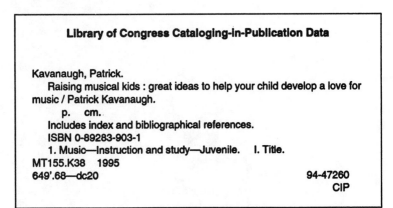

Library of Congress Cataloging-in-Publication Data

Kavanaugh, Patrick.
    Raising musical kids : great ideas to help your child develop a love for
music / Patrick Kavanaugh.
        p.   cm.
    Includes index and bibliographical references.
    ISBN 0-89283-903-1
    1. Music—Instruction and study—Juvenile.   I. Title.
MT155.K38   1995
649'.68—dc20
                                                          94-47260
                                                              CIP

Dedication

◆ ◆ ◆

The book is dedicated to my parents,
Edward and Anne Kavanaugh,
the world's most encouraging,
wonderful parents to ever raise
a musical kid.

Contents

Acknowledgments

◆ ◆ ◆

You will notice throughout this book that I often quote a number of distinguished performers and teachers (both instrumental and vocal). King Solomon once pointed out that there is wisdom to be found in the "multitude of counselors," so I have selected some of those in the profession for whom I have great respect. I have had the privilege of performing with many of these experts through my work in the Christian Performing Artists' Fellowship.

The most prominent musicians I quote throughout this book include:

- Metropolitan Opera star Myra Merritt
- Metropolitan Opera star Jerome Hines (he is also the Director of Opera Music Theatre International)
- Classical guitarist Christopher Parkening
- James Buswell, violinist and string teacher at the New England Conservatory of Music
- Steve Schnurman, tenor and voice instructor
- Anne Williams, principal cellist of the Pittsburgh Symphony Orchestra
- James Kraft, trombonist with the National Symphony
- American Youth Orchestra conductor Luis Haza, also of the National Symphony

But the ideas in this book come from many other sources, including the dozens of teachers with whom I have studied, as well as the hundreds of professional musicians who have discussed these topics with me over the years. My wife, Barbara, an outstanding performer and teacher, is the originator of many of this book's most valuable concepts. And finally, I would like to thank the many, many parents of musical kids whom I have known, who have added many of my favorite parts to this book, and especially my own four young musicians: Christopher, John, Peter, and David.

Introduction

Mozart's Dad

◆ ◆ ◆

E veryone has heard of the great Wolfgang Amadeus Mozart. Whether in movies, books, articles—or through his wonderful symphonies, concerti, operas, or piano pieces—we all recognize Mozart as one of history's most accomplished composers and musicians.

Do you know *why* you've heard of him? Because of a very conscientious dad, namely, *Leopold* Mozart. Although father Leopold was not very talented himself, he was a genius at recognizing and cultivating the talent of his son. He found excellent teachers, enforced many hours of diligent practicing, and arranged Wolfgang's performances all over Salzburg (and later all over the Continent), and... oh, yes, became rather wealthy in the process.

But what if Mozart's parents had never encouraged him in music? Indeed, if his father had not invested years in nurturing the musical aptitude of his talented offspring, little Wolfgang might have become just another obscure kid in the pool halls of Salzburg, and the great Mozart symphonies we all love would never have been composed.

Now, I'm not saying that each of us has a little "Mozart" (but some of us might!). Nor am I simply trying to save your child from the pool halls of your town. But *all* children should have the opportunity to enhance their lives with the joy of music.

I'm not suggesting that we try and force music upon them because we strongly believe it will be good for them. I mean awakening kids—through exposure and encouragement—to the splendor of great music, and seeing them learn to love taking part in it because they really *want* to.

Every child should have the opportunity to have a positive experience in music, to appreciate this marvelous facet of God's creation. Not all children will be musical geniuses like Mozart, or become professional musicians when they grow up. But they all should be allowed the joy of learning how to love great music.

It can happen to any child. I have seen the wildest football fan from the most uncultured background get incurably turned on to Beethoven. I even know former rock-and-rollers who now go to symphony concerts. I have conducted youth orchestras with kids from both the poorest and the richest neighborhoods in town—sometimes sitting together and sharing the same music stand. Music has the ability to bring people from all different backgrounds together. It's wonderful!

Having spent years working with musicians, I've asked many of them—both professional musicians and anonymous but equally appreciative music lovers—how they got turned on to great music. While the details of their stories may differ somewhat between individuals, the stories inevitably revolve around a special person or group of people I've come to call "musical encouragers."

THE MUSICAL ENCOURAGER

Before a child can fully develop his or her God-given musical talents and interests, someone must first create the right environment in which to nurture those gifts. There must be a transfer of the love of music to that impressionable young mind. Someone must take the time and interest to nurture that newly discovered talent, inspire hours of tedious practicing, and provide crucial performance opportunities. Musical encouragers are an integral part of every child's musical development, and they tend to come from two distinct sources:

1. The child's parent(s) and the home environment
2. The child's music teacher(s) and the musical environment

The role of musical encourager is often filled by several people in the course of a child's life. The *key* encourager, however, is always someone very important to the child, someone whom he or she respects. In most situations the encourager is a child's parent or parents.

"But that's impossible—I don't know anything about music!" you may be saying. Don't panic—you probably already act as a "key encourager" in many areas of your child's life that are outside your comfort zone. Whether it's in math, music, or any other specialized subject, it is by your encouraging *attitude* that you help your child.

Most parents of music lovers are not gifted musicians themselves. It isn't necessary to be a music expert to inspire a love for music. The key is to be the right kind of musical encourager.

Neither of my parents had any musical training, talent, or even interest. Yet when I, as a young student, became interested in music, they gave me their wholehearted support. My parents never missed a single concert, and their subsequent praise was fervent and sincere. Night after night they tolerated my incessant practicing and sacrificed without complaint for my musical education. They were truly my first fans.

Likewise, of the many teachers I encountered in the course of my own musical training, there was a very special group I believe were sent from heaven:

- Dr. Conrad Bernier, who, seeing that I was very motivated, gave me four lessons each week without charge.
- Conductor Lloyd Geisler, who constantly gave me his music scores, which I couldn't afford.
- Dr. George Thaddeus Jones, a professor who allowed me to slip unnoticed into his advanced music classes.

To a young musician there is nothing so invaluable as an inspiring, dedicated teacher.

Sadly, I hear of adults who had a strong desire for music as a youth, but were discouraged by insensitive parents. Sometimes I even hear of youths who were turned off to music by apathetic or incompetent teachers who gave lessons only for the money.

And how often do I hear the sad refrain, "If only I hadn't quit my music lessons"? Or even, "How I wish my parents hadn't let me quit my lessons."

Yet I know how challenging it can be for parents to provide their children with a good experience in music. Aside from the financial factors, it takes a lot of energy, motivation, and determination on the part of the parents. And if parents are without proper counsel, it can be very confusing and discouraging when times get tough.

One of the purposes of this book is to provide that counsel, as well as the motivation you will need as you give your children the joy of music.

EVERY FAMILY IS UNIQUE

Those who have read my previous books know that I am a composer and conductor, and have worked with thousands of great musicians. I have also spent many years teaching music to children, from preschoolers to college courses. Working in a number of different academic settings, I even served for several years as the principal of a private Christian school.

Furthermore, I am the father of four fun-loving, high-energy, rough-and-tumble boys. When my kids aren't playing soccer or wrestling with Dad (all five of us on the floor!), we're playing violins and cellos and pianos. I know the needs of parents who want the best for their children because I live every day in that world.

But while every parent wants "the best" for his or her child, this means something different for everyone. Every child God has created is special, with unique needs, backgrounds, and motivations. Not only are your kids unlike mine, but each of your children is different from the others. What works to inspire one child may not always work for another. But if it is presented to them in the right way, music can inspire every child.

WHICH CHAPTERS APPLY TO *YOU*?

Parents need motivation, too. It is marvelous to see the fruit of our efforts, but it can sometimes be a long wait. Through it all we need to keep our eyes fixed on the many benefits we will reap, which is the subject of the first chapter.

The fundamental steps we should take to lead children into a love and appreciation for music are described in chapters 1-5. Once you have used this material to help you discern the individual talents and motivations of your child, the rest of the book is devoted to ideas and guidelines that will help you meet the specific needs of *your* young musician.

Some sections of this book will apply to your situation more than others. If your child is a preschooler, you will want to spend more time in the first few chapters than parents of high school students. The chapters are ordered from younger children to older, but much of the material is applicable for a child of any age.

WHICH GOALS ARE BEST FOR YOUR CHILDREN?

Always keep in mind: Not all of us have the same goals—in fact, we shouldn't. While some proud parents are convinced that their child will be the next Caruso, others simply want to offer a well-balanced background in music for the whole family. Some parents want to cultivate whatever God-given talents their children have. Others would be satisfied to see their child play or sing in church. Still others would like their children to go to college on a music scholarship (they can be quite easy to get, *if* you plan ahead) and pursue music as a career.

This book is designed to help you reach your particular goals for *your* children. I should point out that there are hundreds of examples in this book where, for the sake of simplicity and good grammar I have used gender-specific pronouns such as "he" or "she" (as the father of four boys, I tend to favor "he" over "she"). Please don't be offended or confused by this—the information in this book works equally well with both girls *and* boys.

So as we begin your child's musical odyssey, remember that Sally or Joey does not have to become the next Mozart for musical instruction to have been worthwhile. It will be rewarding indeed simply watching them learn to love Mozart! The joy of music is more than just the finished product—it is also the beautiful process of getting there.

Chapter One

The Benefits of Music for Children

◆ ◆ ◆

"Why should my children study music?"

Ｗe all want the best for our children. And from personal experience, we know that sometimes that will involve a lot of time and hard work. Whatever our children pursue, they are going to need encouragement and motivation along the way.

As a parent and a musician, I believe that the wonderful experience of music is a marvelous way to help our children along that road to adulthood. There are so many benefits of music that can become "transferable skills" for all areas of life. You may already be aware of this and eager to provide that musical experience for your child. Remember, it is a process and even the most enthusiastic of us needs to be reminded of those benefits along the way.

Obviously, if your child turns out to be the next Caruso or Bernstein, you will see clearly the long-term value in providing music for them. But I'm not concerned here about the rewards of a professional musician. Instead, let's focus on some of the advantages the *process* of an education in music can provide every child.

The areas on which I want to focus are:

- Perseverance
- Confidence
- Responsibility
- Identity and Self-Esteem
- Discipline
- A Love of Music, Art, Culture, and History
- Teamwork
- Identification of Talents
- Using Time Wisely
- Following Directions
- Precision and Motor Control
- Overcoming Fears in Public Speaking and Service
- Intellectual and Social Development
- Committment to Excellence
- Creativity and Self-Expression
- Spiritual Nurturing

Some of these benefits may be apparent to you, but others will no doubt surprise you. No matter what aspect of music a child becomes involved with, the benefits of an ongoing exposure to music will help develop qualities in your child's life that will enhance growth in many other areas.

Let's examine the most significant benefits that music can give your child.

PERSEVERANCE (WORKING TOWARD *LONG*-TERM RESULTS)

In the fast-paced society that surrounds our children, everyone is looking for quick, painless results. Yet we as parents know that much of success in life results from perseverance. I am constantly looking for ways to teach this simple but essential principle of achievement to my children.

I believe one of the best ways is through music. From the

time your little Susan sits down with a new piece of music to the time that she can perform it flawlessly (we hope), there may be a long interval. No matter how much inborn talent a child may have, no child is ready to perform a new piece without effort.

And it is this daily commitment to improve, to persevere, whereby music is able to teach a child the indispensable skill of triumphing over large, long-term problems by first dividing them into small sections and conquering them one by one. A three-page composition is set before young David. Today he works on only a few passages, tomorrow a few more, the next day he puts them together, and so on. In the end, what at first seemed difficult to master has now become easy. It is a lesson worth learning as a young child, for I have seen older students and even adults overwhelmed by a large problem because they did not know how to "divide and conquer."

The total process of learning music is a long-term endeavor, and in a way can be appreciated by attending a recital. It is fascinating to attend a recital of violin students of different ages and skill levels. Most programs start with the younger students and their beginning pieces, then gradually proceed to the older ones' more difficult sonatas and concertos. As the level of skill and the growth of years whirl by in the span of an hour, it's like watching a musical time machine.

This picture of growth is also portrayed right before the eyes of the students themselves. As they observe older students who have mastered the same pieces with which they are now struggling, it can be a powerful inspiration toward understanding the importance of perseverance.

CONFIDENCE

As a parent I want my children to succeed in life. I am not as concerned about the specific fields they enter—whether medicine, law, or ministry—but I do want them to know the satisfaction of achievement. To achieve any lasting accomplishment, I am also aware that my children must possess an ample supply of confidence.

Nothing builds confidence better than a successive string of victories, especially when they are progressively challenging. When a great general seems confident in battle against uneven odds, that assurance was usually built by an inspiring track record of prevailing over adversity.

This is exactly what music can provide, even at a very early age. For example, eight-year-old George is given a difficult piece to learn. After an uncertain start and an arduous period of work, he masters it. The sense of accomplishment adds to his self-confidence (especially when accompanied by well-deserved praise), so that George is willing to tackle the next piece of greater difficulty.

Over the years I have seen children with little confidence—especially if they have been unsuccessful in other areas, such as academics or athletics—gradually build self-assurance by conquering one musical piece after another. We as teachers and parents can play an important role in helping to develop a healthy self-confidence, which is essential for any true accomplishment in life.

Incidently, since I brought a military analogy into the world of music, let me give an amusing anecdote about Beethoven's confidence. When he heard of the abusive exploits of Napoleon, the composer exploded, "It's a pity that I do not understand the art of war as I do the art of music—I would conquer him!"

RESPONSIBILITY

Learning an instrument is essentially an independent effort. Even though Mary may have a good teacher and encouraging parents, and belong to fine ensembles, her success or improvement is ultimately up to Mary herself. As we used to say in music school, "In a practice room, it's just *you* and the *piano*."

This new level of personal responsibility quickly becomes apparent to the student. Unlike academic pursuits, which largely involve the simple transfer of factual information, the music student spends hours by himself and is told, in effect, "Improve yourself!"

By mastering musical skills, through patience and perseverance, a child also develops a wonderful by-product: the ability to work by himself to overcome problems. This is an essential element for success in many other areas of life.

I recently heard two somewhat startling statistical facts. Over 90 percent of America's top CEOs and corporate presidents had music lessons in their youth. Over 90 percent of the criminals presently on death row did not!

While I can't guarantee that music will keep your kid off death row, I do know that the diligent pursuit of musical learning will bring him to higher levels of personal responsibility.

IDENTITY AND SELF-ESTEEM

After working with children for years, I have observed that each one needs to seek out his or her area of identity. That discovery of uniqueness is like a personalized badge they can wear that helps to define who they are to those around them. Although the importance of identity is often seen as a phenomenon prevalent among junior-high and high-school students, it is also a factor for children of all ages.

We can't all be the homecoming queen or the star quarterback. But we might be the best cellist, or the student accompanist for the chorus. In most academic and athletic arenas, only the first place is really noticed. Those who place second and third are soon forgotten. Music, on the other hand, has a variety of positions. Your child may not be seen as the school's most talented musician, but may perhaps be recognized and esteemed as the top oboist, the best trombonist, or the one to follow in the alto section.

The Metropolitan Opera star Myra Merritt only began to take voice lessons because she "was bored." When she entered vocal competitions, at first it was only for fun. But when everyone continued to cheer "Bravo!" Myra began to feel differently. She saw music as a part of her self-expression, and started to identify herself as a singer. From that point of identification, it was a short trip to the Met.

Often, children less gifted in academic or athletic fields find their identity in music. An interesting example is Beethoven, who composed huge symphonic masterpieces but never mastered even the most rudimentary skills in arithmetic.

It is also interesting—and wonderful!—to see children with difficult physical handicaps become outstanding musicians. The great violinist Itzhak Perlman was stricken with polio as a young child. Nevertheless, he studied hard on his instrument and has become one of the finest musicians of this century. After he enters the stage on his two aluminum canes and slowly moves toward his seat to perform, his violin explodes with the music of a true master.

No child can be gifted in every area of life, but all children need to feel that they can do something with excellence.

DISCIPLINE

This trait is similar to perseverance in that it is an essential quality for success in the later stages of life. But it's a different skill area that music can help your child to master. Perseverance is the staying power to continue working for years, while discipline (in the musical sense) is the capability to plow through today's little assignment of practicing a small passage—when, frankly, you don't want to.

A violinist friend of mine told of her young daughter struggling to begin her own study of the piano. After weeks of haggling about her daughter's distaste for practicing, my friend exclaimed in frustration, "Anna, don't you want to learn the piano?!" The girl was imperturbable. "No! I want to *play* the piano!"

That's where we *all* are. Thus the need for discipline.

How does music help your child learn discipline? Perhaps by making the process a bit more bearable. I have heard hundreds of musicians tell of the endless hours of tedious practice they endured to learn a certain composition. Yet, their remarks usually sound more like boasting than true complaining. They seem to tacitly testify that the process was actually beneficial.

I would rather practice the same musical passage one hundred times than write the same sentence one hundred times. My perception of improvement, be it ever so gradual, makes each repetition worthwhile. In the meantime, the sound itself continues to affect me with the same delight inherent in all music.

Therefore, learning the discipline of music is a springboard for learning the discipline of any field. We will spend more time on this important topic in chapter seven.

LOVE OF MUSIC, ART, CULTURE, AND HISTORY

Although my expertise is in music, I also see a deep need for children to learn the love of great art and literature. I have found that a Rembrandt portrait or a Dickens novel can strike a chord within me that nothing from the pop culture can stir. And I have noticed that the appreciation of great music is an easy step toward the love of all fine art.

I certainly want my children to learn perseverance and responsibility, as I mentioned before. But I also want them to revel—as I do—in the joy that is the very essence of music. I want them to learn this simple truth: Music really is marvelous, and it's worth listening to!

It is also my desire for my children to have a historical sense of their place in the world. Too many people today seem to know only the present, and have a superficial concept of the past and how greatly it affects us. Great music, spanning the centuries, brings children closer to the eighteenth-century England of Handel, or the nineteenth-century Germany of Mendelssohn.

In our pursuit of shaping the whole child, let us not forget that the appreciation of music and art is a worthy goal in itself.

IDENTIFICATION OF TALENTS

As I mentioned before, I want my children to succeed in whatever fields their talents lie. But how do you discover their hidden talents? They may lie where you least expect.

Since neither of my parents had any noticeable musical talent, a proponent of heredity might not think that their offspring would either. For this reason, it was many years into my schooling before great music was available to me. Yet I took to it like a duck to water and have happily spent my life working in it.

Musical training can also reveal far more than purely musical talent. Those who work with young musicians can quickly note which ones naturally have strong organizational skills, a gift for communication, or have leadership ability.

We want our children to maximize their particular talents, so we begin by helping them to discover what they are. I recommend that parents investigate many nonacademic pursuits, including a wide range of arts and athletics. Although time is needed to see if early obstacles are only temporary challenges to overcome, it doesn't take too long to notice a specific talent or strong interest.

Remember the parable of the "talents" (Matthew 25:14-30). Its lesson is clear: We should never hide our talents. Instead, we should devote our time and efforts to use them and multiply them. But, of course, to use them we first need to identify them.

How about your children? What are their inherent strengths and talents? You'll want to know. So will they.

USING TIME WISELY

There are so many excellent time-management courses offered these days for adults that I'm always surprised how little these basic concepts are taught to children. Yet music is an excellent way to instill the wise use of time into a child's life.

In learning music your child is guided into a situation where he must personally organize great amounts of his time very carefully. This is especially true in learning an instrument through weekly private lessons.

Your son Steven spends six to eight hours a day in school under the time-guidance of the teacher, with only one or two hours of homework where his time-guidance is his own. In contrast, Steven has a one-hour music lesson each week and is left with many hours of practicing—hours for which he is responsible for organizing his own time-guidance. He soon finds out that his musical advancement depends as much on his own management of practice time as on his weekly lesson.

If we want to train our children to use well the irreplaceable time they have, music is a perfect vehicle.

TEAMWORK

When Luis Haza, conductor of the acclaimed American Youth Orchestra, was asked about the benefits of playing in such an ensemble, the first he thought of was "the importance of teaching *teamwork*."

If you think that athletics are the only way to learn teamwork, then you've never played in an orchestra or band, or sung in a good chorus. Although there are many beautiful masterpieces in the solo category, the vast majority of great music is written for combinations of musicians. The great variety of ensemble literature is an excellent illustration of teamwork in action.

Since composers have always been interested in the concept of variety, for centuries they have written music that constantly changes its "star player." For instance, in a given composition, the flute may start with the main theme. A few measures later the violins may pick up the theme, then the clarinets. Of course, the only way to play this effectively is for the instrumentalists to realize that sometimes they play a principal role, and sometimes a supportive one.

In the smaller chamber music ensembles, the students do all the solo vs. secondary support coordination themselves. Even a pianist accompanying a solo singer must learn when to "come out" and when to "lay back," so that the balance between the voice and piano is well executed.

These ensemble techniques between musicians become an excellent method for breaking children out of their innate self-centeredness and making them more aware of the needs of others. Since almost every aspect of life involves working with others, why not teach teamwork to children using the contrasts that composers have woven into nearly every piece of music?

FOLLOWING DIRECTIONS

I recently read that a vast number of young men and women are fired from their first jobs for one reason: failure (or inability) to follow directions. Their dismissal does not mean they were illiterate or even unintelligent. Rather, they simply did not have an ingrained sense of the importance of doing one task at a time, in the proper order, as instructed.

I know of no better way to teach this concept than music. You see, music can *only* be learned step-by-step, in the proper order. You simply can't learn to play anything well without starting with extreme basics; progressing one step at a time, you begin to build musicianship.

Can you imagine learning to play the violin by starting with the colossal Beethoven *Violin Concerto*? There are some areas in life where shortcuts may be possible, but music is not one of them. Even for the child who has been given an enormous amount of inborn talent, each step along the way must be taken in the correct order, or the resulting technique will have holes in it. (The most naturally talented students are simply able to master the steps more quickly than others.)

Mozart may have been a child prodigy, but he still had to learn to follow directions.

PRECISION AND MOTOR CONTROL

"Motor control?" you ask. Too few people realize the importance fine motor control skills will play in a person's life. Yet this ability affects hundreds of activities for the rest of our lives. Every time you sign your name, use a computer or typewriter, even a telephone, you use basic physical skills that require some degree of dexterity.

As sports concentrate on the larger muscles (the "gross

motor skills"), learning to play an instrument is the ultimate in the training of fine motor skills. From the guitar to the piano, the muscles in our all-important fingers and hands are honed to an almost unbelievable precision.

One ironic proof to this muscle training is found when an adult attempts to take up a musical instrument. Now please don't get me wrong here: I strongly encourage *everyone* at any age to begin music! But it is more difficult for an adult's fingers to master the intricate work that little hands seem to get used to quickly.

Furthermore, the importance of exactness and precision—so critical in today's workplace—is a natural by-product of learning music. On a woodwind instrument, for example, the difference between the right note and the wrong one is often a minuscule movement of one finger. For a singer the difference between singing in tune and "off key" is usually a tiny fractional discrepancy of pitch. On a violin this difference can be as small as a $1/64$ of an inch, played with split-second timing—now that's fine motor control!

Since our society demands precision from its workers, and because exactness is best mastered at an early age, music becomes a very effective method for developing it.

OVERCOMING FEARS IN
PUBLIC SPEAKING AND SERVICE

It may surprise you to find that, according to many surveys, the number one fear stated by thousands of people is public speaking. Indeed, for many otherwise happy adults, any kind of public service—especially standing before a crowd—fills them with trepidation. This fear prevents many from taking advantage of excellent opportunities that come their way.

The best way to overcome this fear is by providing non-threatening opportunities to perform. For children this means encouraging them to perform in front of others at an early age—before they even know that they should be nervous! This public exposure is important for all children, but particularly for those who are excessively shy.

As we will discuss in detail in chapter 9, solo performing can be a challenging experience for any child. Of course, an easier starting place for overcoming such fears is in a musical ensemble of some kind. There's safety in numbers, and the shy musician can gradually get used to performing before people. Later, that child can gain enough poise to perform (or speak) in a solo capacity.

Singers have an even greater advantage in this area. Over the years I have noticed that most solo singers are also excellent public speakers. Perhaps the idea of bringing words to a group is already developed within them.

The great Metropolitan Opera star Jerome Hines told me that it was a need to overcome fears that initially drove him into music. As a boy, he was incredibly shy and his parents were quite concerned about this. When they learned that some neighbors were helping their child in this area by sending her to music lessons, they decided to try it with young Jerome. It was like setting a match to gasoline, and within a few years he was singing at the Met!

Your child might not have the same meteoric experience as Hines, but musical training can certainly help cure many such fears. Your child need not be kept from the future opportunities that may come his way—whether singing a solo or giving a speech—by the fears so many adults never overcome.

COMMITMENT TO EXCELLENCE

The notion of excellence is a popular issue these days in the business world in terms of productivity and quality control. But the "quality control," the excellence such as a Pavarotti or a

Toscanini can produce—for which a master-musician strives—is a lifetime, Herculean effort.

One of my favorite Bible verses has always been Philippians 4:8: "If anything is *excellent* or *praiseworthy,* think about such things." True excellence is something we should all strive for, in whatever work we attempt. Certainly, the earlier our children assimilate this principle the better.

With the possible exception of some of the solo events in the Olympics, I know of no better way for children to begin the quest for excellence than with their very first piece of music. One of the reasons for this is that to a practicing musician, every mistake is entirely his own fault. Since there's no one else to blame, overcoming these mistakes becomes exclusively his own achievement.

Of course, there are levels of excellence as a student delves deeper into music. For instance, a beginner at the piano sees perfection as simply not making any mistakes. As Bach once said, tongue-in-cheek, "You simply hit the right notes at the right time and the instrument does the rest." But more advanced students, taking the right notes for granted, strive for correct tempo, phrasing and articulation, and endeavor to infuse the music with their personalized interpretation.

All along this musical road, from the beginner to the pro, there is a constant exertion toward perfection. The training of young musicians to pursue excellence can later be transferred to other areas in their lives. What an incredible world it would be if such a standard for excellence was commonplace in every field!

In closing, the great guitarist Christopher Parkening has some excellent advice for young musicians on the importance of pursuing excellence over success:

Pursue a commitment to personal excellence rather than success, based on your own God-given potential. Success and excellence are often competing ideals. For me, success seeks to please men, but excellence seeks to please God.

Being successful does not necessarily mean you will be excellent, and being excellent does not necessarily mean you will be successful. Success is external—how you have done in comparison to others. Excellence is how you have done in relation to your own potential.

Excellence cultivates principles, character, and integrity. Success may be cheap and you can take shortcuts to get there. You will pay the full price for excellence; it is never discounted. Excellence will always cost you everything, but it is the most lasting and rewarding ideal. What motivates *you:* success or excellence?

INTELLECTUAL AND SOCIAL DEVELOPMENT

There are scientific studies that indicate a possible link between higher intelligence and musical training. Since this is a fairly new field of research, much of the data is still sketchy. Nonetheless, there are many indications that music can affect intellectual development.

Music is one of the few activities that uses both the right and left sides of the brain, as well as the mysterious realm "between" (the *corpus callosum*) that coordinates the two sides. Listening to music is a right-brain activity, while performing, composing, or studying music involves the left side. Thus, music is one of the few common activities that allows children to begin working with both sides of the brain, training it and setting up mental pathways and connections they will use all their lives.

Memory improvement is another area in which music can give your child an advantage. Throughout our lives we are required to memorize huge amounts of data in an organized way that is retrievable. It is no accident that millions of children learn the alphabet by singing the letters to the tune of "Twinkle, Twinkle, Little Star" or that you know the words to hundreds of songs by heart. Music helps our brains organize data. In fact, the process by which your daughter memorizes her music will help her immeasurably to memorize the millions of things—from poetry to telephone numbers—she will encounter in school and throughout her life.

Studies show that even listening to great music can help children in their studies. A 1993 study at the Center for Neurobiology of Learning and Memory at the University of California, Irvine, showed that students consistently scored higher on tests when Mozart was played in the background. Wolfgang would have loved it!

Practical experience has also shown this to be true. It is no surprise that the high school in our area for the gifted and talented students has a great orchestra and chorus. Although there are exceptions—great musicians have undeniably come from a variety of backgrounds—it is rather standard among highly intelligent people to have a deep appreciation of music.

Furthermore, music can be a perfect way to link your children with like-minded peers. If they have a love for music and show talent for learning it, they will want to meet other kids with similar abilities and aspirations. Just as sports-oriented children meet together on various teams, so musical kids meet one another through the learning and performing of music.

CREATIVITY AND SELF-EXPRESSION

Have you ever noticed that when you think of the word *creativity*, you think of the arts almost at the same time? There's a good reason for this association. Creative artists have always been able to express thoughts, feelings, emotions, concerns, and hopes through their art at a level deeper than most of us experience in our day-to-day existence.

I want my children to be able to express themselves fully and creatively. There are so many children (and adults) who have never learned to express their feelings to others. Although the specific field of music may not be everyone's medium for this, there are thousands of children for whom it opens the door of expression as nothing else can.

Certainly this creativity can be seen in those children who are encouraged to compose music. As Beethoven musically expressed the stormy Napoleonic period and Bach musically depicted the devout faith of the German Lutherans, today's musicians learn to express the conviction and feelings within them. I recommend that *all* young musicians be encouraged to compose (more on this topic in chapter 11), although musical creativity is not restricted to composition.

One of the beautiful aspects of performing music is what might be called the "personalized" factor. Why do you think there are different recordings (by many different performers) of the Mozart *Piano Sonatas* at any music store? Each player has his or her own creative style. You'll like one version best; I'll like another. Although the printed music before each musician contains the same notes, there are a myriad of ways to interpret them. Good teachers will inspire their students to look "between the notes" and to put themselves in the music.

This kind of creative spirit, once it is cultivated and developed, can be transferred to many other areas of life. Nearly every profession in the marketplace today is looking for (and generously rewarding) imaginative, perceptive, creative thinkers. William James once said, "Genius means little more than the facility of perceiving in an unhabitual way."

Why not let music find the genius in your children?

SPIRITUAL NURTURING

Throughout my musical career I have heard musicians from a wide variety of beliefs speak of the spirituality of music, of how it seems to break us out of the everyday world.

Since I believe that music is a gift from God, I want to share that gift with my children. I want them to learn how to praise God through music and how to appreciate the beauty of music as a reflection of the creativity of the Lord.

For centuries men and women of faith have used music to express that faith. When Moses triumphed at the Red Sea, his sister Mariam led the nation in an exuberant song of praise and worship to God. When King Jehoshaphat went into battle as instructed by the Lord, he put his musicians in front of the army, proclaiming the praises of God. The many psalms of David, Asaph, and other musicians testify to their faith in the Lord, expressed through music.

Many of the great composers sought to express their convictions through their music. Bach, Handel, Mozart, Mendelssohn, Dvorak, Stravinsky, and many others used music to communicate their deep faith in God, and their work continues to inspire us today.*

In the same way, I want all children to use music to glorify God. They should get involved in the music of their church, both vocally and instrumentally when possible. Since their talents are a gift from the Lord, what better way to thank him than to use those gifts to honor him?

Bach said that the ultimate purpose of music was for the glory of God and the recreation of the human spirit. I want my children to know the joy of using both of these purposes of music.

*For a fuller study of this subject, see my book, *The Spiritual Lives of Great Composers.*

Making It Work for *You* —Try This:

1. To give you some perspective before appraising your children's strengths and weaknesses, consider your own background. Which of the traits listed here came to you naturally as a child? Which of them did you have to work on?

2. Now consider your child (or children, one at a time). What are his (or her) natural strengths? Which of them does he (or she) need to work on?

3. Keep these strengths and weaknesses in mind as you continue through this book. If your children are already studying music, discuss with their teachers what you would like music to accomplish for your children.

Chapter Two

Parents, Kids, and Music Together

◆ ◆ ◆

"How can I prepare my child for a love of music?"

Anyone who has ever had a flower garden knows that a lot of preparation and work must take place long before the flowers bloom in their glory. Likewise, if we want to see the fruit of our children's musical involvement, a certain amount of preparation is necessary. Although other chapters will deal with teachers, schools, and ensembles, this chapter deals exclusively with parents and their children.

I like to think of this musical "seeding the ground" in two broad categories:

1. The parent's role as the childrens' model, and

2. Musical interaction between parents and children.

Although these topics sometimes deal with particular age groups—preschoolers and teenagers have different musical needs—the basic concepts can be applied at any time. For instance, your children, whether they are aged four or sixteen, will learn to love music much more readily if you are a successful role model in this area.

So let's begin in your home, with you. Step-by-step, you can create a nurturing environment for the love of music.

BE A POSITIVE ROLE MODEL

Imagine a parent at the dinner table insisting that his child eat nothing but vegetables while the parent gobbles down a plate of pastry and ice cream. The old adage, "Do as I say, not as I do!" is painfully obvious.

To be able to pass on to our children our love for anything, we must diligently and consistently live it out before them. This applies to music as well.

Being a good role model is simply setting forth a consistent, sincere, non-preachy example that children can routinely see in daily life.

Let's translate this into a musical setting: If you want your children to have a healthy experience with learning to love music, remember that your modeling or at least desiring that same love of music will greatly encourage them in this direction. *Children begin by loving what their parents love.*

When I asked Anne Martindale Williams, principal cellist of the Pittsburgh Symphony, who her first cello teacher was, she had a quick answer. Anne's *mother* was also a professional cellist! Obviously, her mom had modeled a love for music as long as Anne could remember. It is certainly no surprise to find that this daughter has had great success with her music.

But most of us were not so fortunate as to have had such a talented model at home. Being a successful role model does not mean that you must become an expert, but that your children see you demonstrating a sincere interest in music. If your children believe that you want *them* to learn something about which you are personally apathetic, you're going to have an uphill battle. But if they can see that you are genuinely interested in music yourself (and would be even if you didn't have children to influence)—now you're getting their attention!

If you did not have a fulfilling musical experience as a child, don't be discouraged. Developing a love for music can be a wonderful joint venture for you and your family. I already have two children in youth orchestras, yet when I was their age I had never even *seen* an orchestra.

Though you may not have had a musical background, it's your enthusiasm that can make up for any past lack of musical experiences.

CREATE THE RIGHT ENVIRONMENT

For a plant to grow in your garden, it needs more than just water and sunshine. The soil itself has to be robust. In the same way, your child's love of music will flower if his environment is conducive to music and learning.

For most school-age children, their two basic environments are home and school. Let's take time to consider the important part that home life plays in a child's education, whether it involves music or not.

Of the hundreds of children I have met who flourish in music, the large majority come from homes where classical music, great literature, art, and culture are familiar. When the home environment is one of ongoing learning and appreciation for music, the children will want to learn music because they see their parents' *love for learning*. Such adults may be from a wide variety of backgrounds, and have very different interests. Most are fairly well-read, enjoy going to concerts and theater as well as movies, and watch the educational channels at least as much as sit-coms.

This does not mean that all other such activities are wrong or "sub-cultural." Personally, I love football games and we have a pool table in our rec room. (I even have a picture on the wall of Mozart at the billiard table!) But, of course, our lives encompass much more than watching football and shooting pool. And our children observe this every day.

The bottom line is this: Your children need to feel that when they enter into learning music, they are doing something completely *normal*—not something strange and foreign to their home life.

Let me give a few examples that will not drastically alter your life-style, but will provide an atmosphere conducive to musical learning:

- Play classical music quietly (and frequently) in your home and car. Either start a CD collection of great classics or tune to your local classical music radio station. Don't make a big deal about this (never demand silence, or even that they listen), just have it there in the background.

- Let your children see you reading, and not just the newspaper, but *books!* Everyone should have their own tastes, but your children should see that you are trying *new* things, continuing to learn.

  It's wonderfully stimulating when parents discuss (in a light, conversational way) what they happen to be reading with their children—perhaps around the dinner table or in the car. Any time either my wife or I am reading a novel, we keep the kids posted on the action. And a regular opener at dinner should be, "I heard (or read) something interesting today...."

- If you watch TV as a family, don't just tune in Monday Night Football or sit-com family entertainment: check out the educational and arts channels available. The day of the boring educational documentary has finally passed. It's astounding what is being offered today to enrich your lives: orchestras, recitals, opera, concerts of every kind.

- Go regularly to museums, art galleries, historical exhibits, and especially concerts. I have taken our boys right from the soccer field to the art gallery. Believe me, if *you* are excited about it, your children can be too.

Incidently, this modeling is much more successful when it involves both Mom *and Dad*. This is especially true if you have boys in your family. I'm convinced that one of the key reasons boys tend to drop out of music more often than girls is that they see Mom pushing it, while Dad remains inactive. Therefore, the boys see music as a "feminine" thing to do—which is, of course, absurd.

I believe one of the reasons for the musical success of my four boys is that they see big ol' Dad coach their soccer practice, and then go home to play music, or read, or go to a performance. (Sometimes I've even had to conduct an orchestra performance right after coaching!) The appreciation of art, culture, and learning are no more feminine than driving a car is masculine. *Thinking* is something we *all* need to be doing.

The key to creating the right home environment could be spelled out like this:

1. I want my children to learn about music.

2. They will learn much better if they *love* learning about music.

3. They will love learning much easier if they see that *I* love learning about music.

The happiest people in the world are those who keep learning and growing until the day they die. When our children see this positive educational example modeled at home, they will be inspired to *love learning*.

If your home life is naturally filled with opportunities to grow and learn, at least half the battle is already won.

INTERACT MUSICALLY WITH YOUR CHILDREN

Now that the groundwork has been laid, what specific musical things can a parent do with their child? Plenty.

There are lots of things you can do to enhance your child's musical interests and abilities, regardless of your own musical background. Don't feel as though you have to do it all—good music teachers are indispensable. I may have a doctorate in music, but I can't teach my son to play the violin because I don't play that instrument myself. We all have limitations, but your home environment, which is bound to profoundly impact your child's attitudes and values, is yours to create.

The great pianist Glen Gould used to say how much he owed to the fact that he was raised in a house where there was always music. In fact, his mother believed in starting *really* early. While she was pregnant with this future master, she would sit at the piano for hours—for the benefit of his hearing the music in utero!

I realize that most people reading this book are not themselves musicians and may know very little about music. If you know music, fine. But everything I am recommending for parents to do can be accomplished by anyone who is simply willing to invest a little time and effort.

For now, let's look at some types of musical interaction that are very appropriate between all parents and children. Remember that this list is only a beginning, to get you started. Once you begin, let your imagination guide you. The sky's the limit!

FOR INFANTS:

- Play music in the background near them.
- Sing to them.

- Imitate their sounds to them.
- Let them experience many diverse sounds, including any musical instruments in the house.
- Allow them, with supervision, to experiment with a piano or other instruments (not recommended for Stradivarius violins).
- Furnish them with musical toys for their age level.
- Encourage their singing, with and without you.
- Play games singing a known song faster or slower.
- Play games showing loud vs. soft.
- Encourage clapping along to music.
- Roll a ball back and forth with a beat.
- Incorporate movement when listening to music.
- Pretend to play various instruments along with music.
- Play various types of rhythm instruments.

FOR PRESCHOOLERS:

- Continue the appropriate activities previously listed, plus:
- Play "listening games" (for example, drop a spoon away from sight; they must guess what has made the sound).
- Through recordings begin recognition of different instruments and instrumental groups (such as strings, woodwinds, brass, percussion).
- Play games recognizing the different instruments on recordings.
- Explore the differences between singing and speech (for example, sing a song, and then speak the words).
- Play "freeze" with the music (they freeze when they hear a

- Play games trying to match the pitches you sing, or echoing short musical phrases (teach awareness of singing in tune).

- If you have a piano or organ, encourage the child to experiment (improvise) with it.

- Play games clapping a variety of simple rhythms.

- Encourage creative movement to recorded music, perhaps even using props and costumes.

- Practice songs they have learned in Sunday school.

- Begin to teach musical form by singing songs that alternate between verses and a chorus.

- In church show how the notes go up and down in the hymnbooks.

- Show them books that display a variety of musical instruments.

- Read short anecdotal stories about different composers and compositions.

FOR CHILDREN IN ELEMENTARY SCHOOL:

- Continue the appropriate activities from above, plus:

- Listen together to short pieces of recorded music (see Appendix 1).

- Watch short music programs on television together.

- Make up simple songs together (a great way to get children to memorize your "house rules").

- Take them to "kids" concerts (see next chapter).

- Give them short books about music to read.

- Through recordings begin recognition of different periods of music history (such as compositions from the Baroque, Classical, Romantic, twentieth century periods).

- Celebrate the birthdays of great composers (don't forget the cake and ice cream).

- Have children guess how old a certain composer would be if he were alive today.

- Encourage improvisation at the keyboard or other instrument.

- Make home recordings of their musical efforts (great gifts for grandparents).

FOR HIGH-SCHOOL STUDENTS

- Continue the appropriate activities previously listed, plus:

- Encourage them to help select new CDs for the family.

- Encourage them to read about music and the great composers.

- Relate the history of music to the events occurring at the same time in non-musical history.

- Give them a recording of their favorite composer for birthdays or other special days.

- Give musical gifts—you can get everything from Bach handbags to Mozart sweatshirts from your local music store or through catalogues.

- Encourage true composition; have their improvisations written down and polished.

- Take them to serious concerts (see next chapter).

- Take them to see and even meet with famous musicians.

- Arrange to meet with a living composer (check at the local college's music composition department).

Making It Work for *You* —Try This:

1. Give yourself a quick evaluation as a role model. Do you want to continue to learn? Do you have an interest in music? Remember: children begin by loving what their parents love.

2. Find the classical music radio stations in your area and quietly play good music in your home and car, from the radio or recordings.

3. Consider your home and your life-style. Is it conducive to music and to learning? Find time this week (how about tonight?) to *interact musically* with your children.

Chapter Three

Take Your Children to Concerts

◆ ◆ ◆

"How can I best expose my children to great music?"

Buying CDs (and listening to them) is important. But if you are going to turn on children to music, one of the most effective ways is to attend concerts. Even with all the marvels of today's recording technology, there's still no substitute for the thrill of a live performance. But before you bundle your children up and head out the door to a live concert, there are a number of points to consider. When I think of taking children to concerts, I think of four important questions:

1. Which concerts should we attend?
2. What preparation is helpful beforehand?
3. What should we be doing during the performance?
4. What can I do afterward to confirm the positive experience?

Let's take them one at a time.

WHICH CONCERTS SHOULD WE ATTEND?

When trying to decide which concert to attend with your children, be sure to take into consideration critical factors such as the ages of your children, their interests and attention spans, your personal tastes, what you can afford, and of course, the limits of your area's selection.

Obviously, the number one limitation for many is location. Parents in New York City have a greater variety of concerts to choose from this weekend than parents in rural areas. But very few people are totally isolated from some type of music performance. With new orchestras and ensembles forming everywhere, this situation gets better every day.

How do you find out what's available near you? In *A Taste for the Classics,* I listed six basic ways to become aware of the live music performances in your area:

1. Check the newspaper regularly, especially on the weekends.
2. Listen to the radio and TV for advertisements and information.
3. Get on the mailing lists of any performing organizations you discover near you.
4. Buy subscription seats each season to your favorite group.
5. Check with local music schools or the music departments of local colleges for their performance schedules.
6. Seek out music teachers and local amateur music groups.

I strongly recommend that parents try one or all of the above to determine which upcoming musical events are in their area. When you have done this, you should have at least a few good options from which to choose.

Many music organizations (orchestras, opera companies, and so forth) have "kiddie concerts," and these can be wonderfully entertaining. They usually consist of short, exciting pieces and often involve a narrator who verbally elucidates the message of the music. Whether through school field trips or in families, take advantage of these educational opportunities whenever they occur.

Your child's experience, however, doesn't have to be confined to "kiddie concerts," if you pick your performances carefully. Consider a few key words: short, fast, loud, exciting, contrasts, and visual appeal.

Although a few stuffy musicologists don't like to admit it, most kids respond to music that is fun and exhilarating, which usually translates to fast, loud, and with a lot of colorful contrasts. This attraction to musical contrasts usually necessitates a lot of different kinds of instruments. Therefore, a full orchestra is probably going to capture a child's interest more than a string quartet, which is rather an acquired taste.

Furthermore, the more that happens visually—the movement of the strings in an orchestra, an exciting soloist, a captivating opera scene, or even ballet—the more likely your child will respond to the music.

And, of course, with children (and many adults), short is beautiful. Not necessarily short concerts, but short movements of music. If a concert itself is too long, you can leave, or arrive, at intermission. For a young child this is something worthy of consideration.

Because every child's attention span is different, the length of the concert is something to consider. I have seen spellbound youngsters and fidgety adults. But in general, the younger the child, the shorter the attention span. Hence the need for short movements and many breaks.

Here are a few guidelines for selecting your next concert outing:

- Orchestra concerts are very good, especially if the program has several shorter pieces rather than one or two long ones.

The music from the late nineteenth and early twentieth centuries will have enough contrasts and orchestral color to hold a child's attention.

- A concert with a concerto using a child's favorite instrument is a wonderful choice. This way, you get this fascination of the orchestra plus the Olympic-like excitement of a spectacular soloist playing an instrument with which the child is already familiar.

- A program of staged opera *scenes* can be very effective. These excerpts can give a child the best of music with the best of theater, especially if the scenes are sung in English.

- The ultra-visual ballets will always be popular with children, especially if they are in short sections with a strong story line. It's no coincidence that Tchaikovsky's *Nutcracker Suite* ballet sells out each year.

- You may want to wait before bringing children to most chamber music and solo recitals (due to the lack of instrumental contrast), as well as choral music concerts (because of the length of most choral repertoire). I love them deeply, but they are generally hard for children to appreciate.

HOW SHOULD WE PREPARE BEFOREHAND?

Once you have selected a concert to attend, there are several things you can do beforehand that will add to your children's perception of the music they will hear. With a little time and effort, you can prepare your children by gathering information in the following areas:

1. the performers or type of ensemble in this concert,
2. the composer(s), and
3. the music itself.

To illustrate this, I'll share how I often go about selecting a program that might benefit some of my children. I pick up my local newspaper (I live near Washington, D.C.), and browse through the arts and entertainment section.

Hmmm... here's one that looks interesting. The classical gui - tarist Christopher Parkening is playing a concerto with the National Symphony on March 17, 18, 19, and 22. Since the shows on the first three nights are at 8:30 p.m.—and my kids' manners tend to go downhill if they stay up too late—I think we will try the show on the 22, which is at 7:00 p.m. Pardon me while I order a few tickets.

The performers. Since a concerto involves both an orchestra and a solo instrument, I need to make sure the younger children are enlightened about both. Some evening this week, I will take our younger two boys (ages four and seven) through a little book with pictures of all the orchestral instruments. Perhaps we will play some games about recognizing the sounds of different instruments on a recording or the radio. (Be sure to do this alone at first to make sure *you* can distinguish the different instruments yourself.)

The concert I picked this time has a guitar soloist. These days, it's safe to assume that all kids know what a guitar is, even a classical guitar. Still, we might talk around the dinner table about the difficulties of playing this instrument, the reasons for the popularity of the guitar, and so forth. I make it a point to play classical guitar recordings throughout the house during the week of the concert.

The composer(s). In this concert Parkening is playing a piece called the *Concierto de Aranjuez*, by Joaquin Rodrigo. A quick peek through a music reference book (see appendix 2) tells me that this work was written in 1930 by a blind Spanish composer, and that it is the most popular guitar concerto in the repertoire. This week we may look a bit at Spanish history and culture, or discuss around the table how a blind man could write music.

The music itself. The most important preparation you can make for a concert of any kind is to *hear* the music first. This often means running out to the local library or music store to find a CD, but this gives you a good excuse for building up your CD collection anyway.

This may surprise you, but I don't recommend that you force your children to sit still and listen to the entire CD with you. Without visual stimulation, most children will soon become bored, fidgety, and often resentful. We may listen to parts of it together, but I prefer to simply play it in the background repeatedly, casually reminding them that this is the piece we get to hear next week at the concert.

Since I want them to remember it well, I'd better listen to it myself and be able to make comments. Then, while it plays at dinner time, I can seed the conversation with, "Here comes that incredibly fast passage," or, "I think it's fascinating how the strings imitate the guitar here," or, "Listen to how high those guitar notes are."

Let me give you an important equation:

$$\frac{\text{Your personal enthusiasm} + \text{Repeated listenings}}{\text{Children's musical recognition}}$$

You'll be amazed at how much they can remember. During the actual performance, you'll get a sidelong glance and an excited smile every time the soloist plays that fast passage you commented on at dinner the week before.

AT THE PERFORMANCE

Your top priority the day of the performance is to make it a fun, positive experience for your children. Think of things that they like which will add to their enjoyment. Whether it's a special breakfast or stopping for ice cream on the way home, this should be remembered as a special day.

Dress should be casual and comfortable. I know that you don't want them in ragged sweat pants, but restrain the urge to dress them up too much. I have seen too many miserable children pulling at their tight ties during a long program. We don't want to start off their positive day with arguments about their clothes.

The trip to the concert hall is an important time to discuss what they are about to see and hear. Ask questions that will get their imaginations going: "Do you think the performers are getting nervous?" "How would you feel if you were about to perform for all those people?" Always tell them that afterward each child will tell about his or her favorite part, and remind them of the need for silence during the performance.

Make sure you arrive early enough to have all children visit a restroom before the concert begins. It's not much fun when, in the middle of a performance, little Billy looks at Mom or Dad imploringly and they have to entertain (or disturb) the entire audience by their very noticeable exit.

When you arrive at the hall and find your seats, quickly glance through the program notes in the printed program the ushers will give you. You may find some interested information about the music, composer(s), or performer(s) that you can tell your children before the concert starts.

Once the music begins, silence should be absolute. In modern concert halls, scientific advances in building acoustics will make even a tiny whisper heard by many people around you.

I'm afraid that chewing gum and candy wrappers should also be left at home. Remember, those people near you also paid their hard-earned money to hear this concert—not to be distracted by noisy children.

I might as well say something here that may be unpopular with a few proud parents. Babies and concert halls don't mix. No matter how beautiful your little baby is, the enforced silence of a concert hall is no place for an infant. In many halls today, ushers, required by the management, will ask you to leave the hall at the baby's first peep. In fact some halls will not allow babies to attend concerts with parents. So you may want to hire a baby sitter. Sorry. They'll grow up soon, and the concerts will still be there.

If concert-going is new for you, remember *not* to applaud between different movements of the same piece. Wait for the entire work to conclude and then join in with the rest of the audience.

At every applause you have a moment to talk quietly. This is your chance to show enthusiasm and to ask questions that might add to your children's perception of the music. Ask a few thought-provoking questions: "Did you notice when...?" "Did you hear the...?" "Could you tell when the music did...?"

At intermission get out of those chairs and stretch the legs. (As if your children would sit there for long anyway!) Walk around the hall, go upstairs, sidestage, anywhere they will let you go. A concert hall can be a very interesting place.

Also during intermission make a judgment call concerning the energy and interest of your children. I know that you paid for the *whole* show, but it would be better to leave now with a positive experience than to wear them out and finally leave with grumpy, unappreciative children.

Some parents have found success in longer concerts by bringing paper and pencils for the children. The older children can write a story about the music, the younger ones can draw a picture. This can be done with the right preparation and materials. Remember, a concert hall is not a classroom. Any sounds of tearing paper, turning pages, or dropping pencils, and the storm-troopers—I mean ushers—will be on their way.

AFTER THE CONCERT

After the performance is over and the applause has died away, there are two things I recommend to confirm the positive experience for your children. First, while the excitement is still with us, let's head backstage and meet the artists.

"What?!" asks the exhausted Mom, who feels that she has now paid her dues to motherhood and wants to get her crew in the car and head home. I know you're tired, but this will be well worth it. In fact it can be as important and memorable as the concert itself.

In some concert halls it can be quite an adventure to find the way to backstage, the "Green Room" (reception room), or the stage door. Ask an usher for directions. Hurry, not only to beat the crowds but to increase your childrens' eagerness level.

If your concert included a soloist, there may be a line to wait in, but it goes quickly. Believe me, meeting a famous soloist or conductor, shaking his hand, and getting an autograph (a must!) can be an experience your child will remember for years to come. Kids love to get autographs and performers love to give them. An autographed program is a trophy for your child to proudly take home, as thrilling as a top baseball card. I still treasure an autograph of the great guitarist Andrés Segovia I got while in high school, after standing for two hours in the snow following a winter concert. You never know how such encounters can inspire a young musician.

Cellist Anne Martindale Williams tells with enthusiasm how, as a young musician, she saw the cellist Jacqueline du Pré perform. As Anne watched the power and energy that exuded from du Pré's instrument, she was herself inspired to become a great cellist. Indeed, almost all performers were at one time inspired by contact with other great performers.

But don't just go to meet a featured soloist. Even if your concert didn't have a particular soloist and if the conductor is unavailable, mingle around backstage and meet some of the members of the orchestra. Treat all the musicians with respect. Remember, the Bible says to "show proper respect to everyone" (1 Pt 2:17). This means everyone, not just the world-famous soloists.

HOME AGAIN

This is a good time to use your children's enthusiasm to discuss what they just heard. And sure enough, I have some questions for you to critique the performance with your children. Try to keep the conversation interesting and very positive.

My favorite types of critique questions are those that use the word *favorite*:

- "What was your favorite piece? Why?"
- "Describe your favorite section of the music."
- "What was your favorite instrument? Why?"
- "Who is now your favorite composer? Why?"

Children also love the "review" questions:

- "Who can remember every piece played in the concert?"
- "Who can remember every composer played in the concert?"
- "Who can remember the name of the soloist(s)?"

- "Who can remember the name of the conductor?"
- "How many instruments can you name that were played?"

And don't forget the thought-provoking questions, like:

- "What did the music in your favorite piece convey?"
- "How would you compare the different pieces?"
- "In what ways were the pieces all very different (or very similar)?"
- "What did you notice that was special about this concert?"

Whether such dialogue takes place on the drive home, later that night, or through the week, the parent's attitude makes all the difference. This is your chance to find out what's inside your children and to help them express their feelings. As exhausting as a concert day can sometimes be—especially for a large family—you'll know that you made a difference as you tuck one of your little ones into bed and hear, "Daddy, when can we go to another concert again?"

Making It Work for *You* —Try This:

1. Check out the TV listings this week for a great concert to watch together. (This may be a good "trial run" for your kids before attending a live concert.)

2. Find out what performing ensembles are in your area. Check out the newspaper (arts section) and yellow pages, and call various radio stations.

3. Ask some of your acquaintances who might know about concerts in your area.

4. Plan a concert outing today. It may not take place for weeks, but start planning for it now. You'll be glad you did, and so will your children.

Chapter Four

Vocal or Instrumental?

◆ ◆ ◆

"Where is the best place to start my child in music?"

In a concert hall there are two kinds of people: those on the stage (who perform) and those in the audience (who listen). In the previous chapter I encouraged everyone to go to concerts with their children, getting them into the audience. Now, let's begin to lead your child from the role of spectator into that of participant.

I firmly believe that every child needs some hands-on music experience. This experience can come in a wide variety of ways, but ultimately, the two categories in which a child can participate in music are vocal and instrumental. All music is divided into these two categories.

Should your child sing or play an instrument? Let me answer emphatically in one word: both!

This certainly does not mean I advocate regular private lessons in both voice and an instrument. But I do mean that every child ought to have the opportunity to learn an instrument and that every child needs to sing, at least in some capacity.

First of all, *everyone* needs to sing, whether in the shower or in a church choir. The English composer William Byrd summed it up almost four hundred years ago: "Since singing is so good a thing, I wish all men would learn to sing."

Singing has been an integral part of every culture throughout history. From the time we hear (and try to imitate) our first lullaby until a hymn is sung at our funeral, singing is and should remain a part of everyday life.

When the psalmist exhorts us to "sing unto the Lord," I'm sure he didn't mean once each week at church. Singing should so permeate our life-style that it can happen almost anywhere, at almost any time.

Furthermore, each child should learn at least one instrument with some proficiency. Studying an instrument is the best way to begin an active participation in music. Such an experience can deepen Johnny's love of music—and therefore the joy he will receive through music—for the rest of his life.

The psalmist also exhorts us to "play skillfully," and that will necessitate the diligent study of an instrument.

Well then, vocal and instrumental. Which should come first?

Although any opportunities to sing—whether at home, school, church, or in public—should be encouraged, I do not recommend *studying* singing for young children. Vocal training is better left to the high school years, beginning at ages twelve to fourteen for girls and fifteen to sixteen for boys. Indeed, many young voices have been damaged by pushing them too hard too soon.

Even if you have enthusiastic aspirations for your children to be singers, let them first learn an instrument. It will greatly help them in their singing someday. In fact most of the great singers I have met have also played instruments. And most of the great instrumentalists I know love to sing.

I will deal with the many aspects of vocal training later in this book. For now we will enter the incredible world of instrumental music. The purpose of this chapter is to help you make the necessary decisions about your child learning an instrument.

The first question we must ask ourselves is, "*Which* instrument should my child learn?" This question is fundamental, whether your child is in a school music program, takes private music lessons, or is taught by a parent.

Before we consider the various possibilities for your child, I want to deal with an important question: "Should all children learn, at least at first, the *piano?*"

THE PIANO: NECESSITY OR LUXURY?

There are some convincing arguments for the "piano first" advocates, which you should consider for your children:

- The initial reward is almost immediate. That is, *anyone*, even a baby, can push down the keys of a good piano, and it sounds remarkably like a good piano! This is in great contrast to the first scratchy sounds of a violin or the first wretched screeches of a trumpet. The piano sounds great immediately, which can be quite motivating for younger students.

- The piano is a very visual instrument. Children can "see" many aspects of music, which will make the explanation and learning of these musical concepts easier. The lower and higher pitches of music are clearly seen from the left to right on the keyboard. Intervals, chords, melody vs. harmony, and many other important elements of music are easily understood and can then be transferred to different instruments at a later date.

- Pianists don't need an accompanist. They can do it all themselves. Unlike monophonic instruments such as the woodwinds and the brasses, which produce only one tone at a time, the piano can produce as many sounds as you can play simultaneously.

  There is nothing quite like the joy of sitting down at the piano and playing a lovely composition in its entirety. The great composer Franz Josef Haydn reflected, "When I sit at my old worm-eaten piano, I envy no king in his happiness."

- There are more teachers for the piano than any other instrument. This alone can be a deciding factor if you live in a small town, where an oboe or french horn teacher might be difficult to find.

- There is a vast quantity of magnificent piano literature. From Bach to Bernstein, nearly all the great masters composed reams of piano music, including some excellent pieces for students. Furthermore, piano (or at least "keyboards") are employed in virtually every style of music.

- A piano is relatively easy to maintain by having it tuned about twice a year; dusting I leave to your discretion. A piano is hard to damage with anything much smaller than an axe, and can be a fashionable addition to your house. A piano can be obtained at a reasonable price, or even rented. If, later on, you want to sell it, there usually is someone ready to purchase it.

- Piano technique, though different from that of the organ or harpsichord, is easily transferred to all keyboard instruments, including electronic ones.

Though there are many positive reasons for your child to begin piano, I want you to also be aware of some of the limitations of studying piano:

- Piano playing lacks the many benefits of a group experience. One of the advantages I have already mentioned is that the piano's many notes can "do it all," without the need of other instruments. This feature can be a great drawback, especially for peer-oriented children.

    Thousands of talented young pianists have taken lessons for years, and performed in many solo recitals, yet have *never* played in a musical ensemble. This lack of group participation can be *very* discouraging for the youngster who wants to play with others. One of my sons, for example, miserably endured many months of piano lessons, complaining of the enforced solitude: "This is like playing with a soccer ball, only by yourself!" Later, we moved him to violin, where he has flourished. He especially enjoyed the fun of playing in a youth orchestra and other ensembles with his peers.

- Because young pianists almost never play their instrument with other musicians (except in a duet written for four hands), inaccuracies in their playing are often not corrected. When you're playing a solo, if you slow down or speed up, it doesn't affect anyone. You don't have to follow anyone else, or even listen to anyone else. There are many fine young pianists who sound wonderful with their solos, but are incapable of playing in groups. They have lived in their own little musical world so long that they have a difficult time realizing that all music does not revolve around their piano.

- The very size of a piano presents an obvious limitation. It is not very mobile. Therefore, if a pianist goes somewhere and wants to play, there had better be a piano already there—preferably well in tune and in good condition. Pianists are often jealous of other instrumentalists who never go anywhere without their violin, horn, or flute.

- A piano, like any other instrument, takes years in which to gain even a basic proficiency. Therefore, if you subscribe to the common idea of "a background in piano before starting an orchestral instrument," the time involved could place your child several years behind those students who went directly to a violin or flute.

Certainly, this time is not wasted, but it can be discouraging to a student who finally enters an ensemble—only to find that his friends are far more advanced because they were playing their instruments those years while he was at piano lessons. This was made clear to us when our son, after all his piano lessons and then two years of violin, joined a youth orchestra at age twelve. Imagine his incredulity when the first violinist was a girl of seven—who had been playing violin for five years.

- Because the piano is so universally popular, the competition factor is greater than with any other instrument. In 1985 the American Music Conference of Chicago, Illinois, surveyed the use of music instruments by amateurs. They found that there are over twenty million pianists in America, compared to four million on either the flute or clarinet, and only 2.3 million violinists.

   In school, this means that it is very hard to be the best pianist. In the professional music world, especially since the piano is not used in a symphony orchestra, very, very, *very* few pianists can make a living as a performer.

So, what is the answer to the great piano debate? Let me leave you with three points to ponder:

1. Learning piano as a child can be a wonderful experience, but it is *not a necessity*. It has advantages and disadvantages, and will depend much upon the personality and aspirations of each child. Of my four children, all are musically inclined, but only two have specifically taken piano lessons.

2. The one exception to this guideline has to do with singers. I know that the subject of singers is saved for a later chapter, but since we're on the subject of piano, I must mention: *ALL* singers need to learn the piano. No exceptions. The piano will help them learn their music, and it will enable them to visualize the pitches they are singing. Besides, it's a lot cheaper than hiring an accompanist.

3. Although I don't recommend piano lessons for every child, I strongly recommend that every family own a piano—or at least some keyboard instrument. When your young cellist, trombonist, or clarinetist needs an accompaniment, what can he do without a piano nearby? Even young violinists and flutists can find delight walking past a keyboard and playing a few tunes.

For centuries the keyboard has come to represent a major part of the musical art, and it's great to have one around. In 1870 Ralph Waldo Emerson aptly commented, "'Tis wonderful how soon a piano gets into a log hut on the frontier."

Making It Work for *You* —Try This:

1. Talk to your young child about the differences and similarities of singing versus playing an instrument.

2. See if your child can match pitches with you, and then melodies. Sing a note and ask her to sing the identical note. Then sing a short melody and ask her to sing it back to you on the same pitches.

3. If you have a piano, sit at it frequently with your child—even if you have no keyboard experience yourself. Does she like to play around with the keys, or is she immediately bored? A child's interest in an instrument is one good indication of his or her aptitude for it.

Chapter Five

Strings, Winds, and Percussion

◆ ◆ ◆

"What are the disadvantages of each instrument?"

N ow that we have dealt with the piano, let's look at the variety of other instruments from which to choose. We will examine them within their orchestral groupings: strings (that is, "bowed" strings), woodwinds, brass, percussion, and "other" (for such instruments as the guitar and organ).

STRING INSTRUMENTS (VIOLIN, VIOLA, CELLO, BASS)

Praise him with the strings.   **Psalm 150:4**

The strings are the one musical family that kids can grow into. For instance, they may start on a 1/8 size violin, then grow into a 1/4 size, then a 1/2 size, a 3/4 size, and finally graduate to a full-sized violin. This "growing instrument concept" applies to all four of the strings and lends itself well to young students, whose hands and fingers are constantly growing during childhood.

There is almost *always* a shortage of string players (especially violinists) in every school and every orchestra, so if your child wants to feel needed, encourage him to pick a string instrument. It's the old law of supply and demand. A typical orchestra needs two or three flutes. Orchestras seldom require more than four wind instruments of any kind. But they need over *thirty* violins, plus about a dozen violas, another dozen cellos, and eight to ten basses. It's nice not to have all the ultra-competition that the pianists have. And even as a child, it's nice to feel needed.

By selecting a string instrument for your child's first instrument, you are opening up endless opportunities for musical experience, both present and future. If your child's interest and skill level reach a high level of proficiency, it can be a relatively easy way to get a college scholarship since so many string players are needed in every college orchestra. If you're any good, you can make a decent living playing a string instrument.

On the other hand, elementary and high school orchestras (if they exist at all) often play second fiddle (sorry about the pun) to the school band. A band has no place for string players, except for an occasional use of the double bass to support the lowest notes. (Outnumbered at least fifty to one, this bass player *really* looks like he walked into the wrong rehearsal!)

This "orchestra vs. band" factor may play a part in your child's school someday. If your school has a big orchestra, your talented violinist might be the most popular kid on campus. If they only have a band, the same violinist might be the loneliest kid on campus.

It should be noted that in an orchestra the string players all play together as a section. This means that they seldom have the solos that woodwind and brass players take for granted. Some extroverted children might be appalled at this prospect; you'd better give them a trumpet. Other children will actually find security in being part of a large string section.

A *very* big plus for learning strings is the wonderful repertoire, perhaps second only to that of the piano. Composers for centuries have specialized in writing for strings and giving the strings the primary place in the orchestra. The huge bulk of chamber music is for strings, particularly the beautiful repertoire of the string quartet. The many violin and cello sonatas, as well as concertos, written by the masters are incomparable and often transcribed for other instruments. String players have never lacked for great music.

One negative (and often joked-about) aspect of learning strings is that the first year or two can be somewhat rough on the ears—I mean the parents' ears! It takes a while for the child to gain enough control of the bow (right-hand technique) to avoid an assortment of squeaks and scratches. Furthermore, unlike the guitar—which has frets to mark the finger placement—these stringed instruments provide no indication of where to place your fingers. The resulting notes of a beginner can be rather out of tune.

Though these first few years of a string instrument may require a lot of patience and encouragement for your child, the rewards are worth the wait.

The violin. The violin is the king of the string instruments, with the majority of melodies and preeminence. It is one of the oldest instruments still in use today and one of the few that has undergone only minor structural changes over the centuries. Among the hundred or so musicians in a modern orchestra, the chief violinist (called the "concertmaster") is second in command to the conductor. (In fact, if the conductor is inept—and this does happen—players in the orchestra begin to ignore him and follow the concertmaster.)

In an orchestra the violins are divided into two sections, the "first violins" and the "second violins." Although most music calls for good players on *both* parts, the "firsts" generally play the most prominent and demanding music. Therefore, an inexperienced student will usually be given a chair toward the back of the "seconds." As the student's skill improves, he or she usually can audition to try and advance to the "firsts."

The viola. Usually, those who play the slightly larger viola began as violinists, as they use similar technique. Often, the switch to viola is prompted by a desperate school orchestra conductor who is ready to pay any price to get a few violas. Many professional players "switch-hit" all their lives on these two instruments; you can get twice as many paying jobs!

I don't think anyone "switch-hits" between the cello and bass. Although they often play the same musical part in an orchestra, they are two very different instruments.

The cello. If the violin is the king of the musical chessboard, the cello (pronounced CHEH-low) is the queen. Because of its extreme range from very low notes to very high, the cello is a beautiful and versatile instrument. Therefore, cellists actually get more solos than their neighbors on either side (violas or basses).

Cellos are a little heavier to carry than either violins or violas, of course, but loyal cellists never complain about it. A cartoon in my wife's cello studio shows a storm at sea with a ship sinking in the background. In the foreground are two men in the ocean clinging to their floating cello cases and asking one another, "I wonder how the piccolo player is making out."

The double bass. The double bass (or contrabass, or simply "bass") is the largest of all the string instruments. (The musical bass rhymes with "case.") Historically, the bass is also not related to the violin, viola, or cello, and is tuned differently. Bass players may not get many solos, but all orchestras need them. They play an important role with their low range by providing those foundation notes necessary for many compositions. They also have the odd advantage of being able to switch over to the electric bass guitar and make a few extra dollars playing jazz. (Not too many cellists would try this.)

WIND INSTRUMENTS

Praise him with the sounding of the trumpet... and flute.
Psalm 150:3-4

If the strings provide your children with the joy of feeling needed, the winds provide a joy that most string players seldom experience: solos! While the strings always play together as a section in an ensemble, the winds often get to play beautiful solo passages.

Playing a wind instrument in an orchestra is a bit like playing on a baseball team: There is a lot of waiting, then suddenly you're at bat (or playing an exposed solo) and everyone is watching you (or listening to you).

Of course, winds also play in sections, too, and in bands their parts are often doubled—or tripled—for extra volume and richness. But let's face it, the flute or trumpet has a lot more chances to play a solo than a viola or cello. In the eyes of many children and parents, this is a great plus for learning a wind instrument.

Another benefit to wind instruments is the relatively short amount of time needed for some positive results. After one or two lessons Lucy can blow into a flute, move a few fingers, and the result sounds remarkably like a flute. Granted, she doesn't yet sound like Jean-Pierre Rampal or James Galway, but she's probably a lot more in tune than her friend Sue—who's still playing open strings on her violin.

Wind instruments (except for the trombone) come already tuned, or at least fairly tuned. My friends who are professional wind players know better than this; to truly play with expertise, they are constantly aware of miniscule adjustments to playing perfectly in tune. But for beginners, winds are wonderfully in tune, especially compared to the non-fretted strings.

In effect, George is given a trumpet and told that if he blows in the mouthpiece and pushes the right button (valve), middle C will come out. He does as instructed, and to his delight— and probably his parents' astonishment—middle C emerges! Of course, they may be hearing it for the rest of the evening.

A very practical advantage for wind instruments is the price tag. As a general rule winds simply do not cost as much as string instruments. This becomes especially true as the student becomes more musically advanced and needs a better instrument. Compared to the many thousands one can pay for a professional-quality violin or cello, even the best wind instruments seem reasonable.

Good student instruments for your son Billy can be found for excellent prices. Do some shopping around; you may even be able to find a used instrument in excellent condition. Let's worry about the price of professional-quality instruments later. Better yet—why not let little Billy worry about that someday when he's older.

In case you haven't noticed, all the woodwinds aren't made of wood, only the oboe, clarinet, and bassoon. Many years ago the flutes were wooden too, and when they started being made of silver, they were already card-carrying members of the woodwinds. Later, when Adolph Sax invented the saxophone in 1840, its construction and fingering system was so woodwind-like (especially clarinet-like) that it joined the club, too.

Woodwind players have the fascinating distinction of having "big brother" (or "little brother") instruments on which they often perform. For instance, a flutist is occasionally asked to play the piccolo, a little "baby flute," sounding an octave higher. The oboist also plays the larger English horn, and the bassoonist plays the much larger contrabassoon. The clarinets and saxophones each have their own families (alto sax, bass clarinet, etc.) and can switch from one to another fairly easily.

In each case the fingering for the primary instrument is the same for its auxiliary instrument. Except for a little size adjustment, covering the same holes produces the same notes. So if you can play a flute, you can play a piccolo—at least in principle. It's like learning two for the price of one!

The flute. The woodwinds are sorted into interesting categories. The preeminent flute, queen of the winds, has a unique construction. It has neither a mouthpiece on which to place your lips (like the brasses) nor a mouthpiece inserted into the mouth (like the other woodwinds). Instead, its air column is activated by blowing *over* a hole in the flute similar to the notes produced by blowing across an open cola bottle. Try it sometime.

Because of this simple technique, or because it is the highest woodwind with the majority of solos—or perhaps because of its lovely, clear tone—the flute has always been *very* popular. This provides Lucy lots of flute-playing friends—especially if she is in a band program where flutes come in droves—as well as lots of competition. As always, whether this is an advantage or a disadvantage will depend on the individual child.

The clarinet and the saxophone. Two woodwinds which go hand in hand are the clarinet and the saxophone. These are called "single-reed" instruments because their mouthpieces contain a wooden reed that is vibrated in order to produce sounds. The fingerings are so similar that—like the violin and the viola—many clarinet players "double" on the sax, and vice versa.

Both the saxophone and clarinet are quite versatile and are used in many different styles of music. Consequently, these two are also very popular, and in bands they sometimes surpass the number of flutes. Of course, the clarinet is used more often than the saxophone in an orchestra. But the sax makes up for this with its frequent employment in jazz and "pop" music. And it should be noted that the saxophone can be a *very* lovely instrument playing the classical music of the last century.

The oboe and the bassoon. Next are the "double-reed" instruments, the oboe and the bassoon. The mouthpieces of these instruments contain double reeds that vibrate to produce pitches. Considering the rich beauty of their distinctive sounds and the thousands of wonderful solos in the standard repertoire, I have always been surprised at their lower popularity with children. Music teachers have told me that it's because these instruments are initially harder to play than the other woodwinds. It is my opinion that they are simply too beautiful as musical instruments to quickly dismiss, even at an early age.

Since the other woodwinds are more popular at first, the young oboist or bassoonist has the marked advantage of lower competition. At an audition to pick two of each woodwind instrument, you may have three or four bassoons trying out— compared to several dozen clarinets! If one of my sons wants to learn a woodwind instrument, I'm going to encourage him to play one of the double-reeds.

Remember the "supply and demand" principle I mentioned with strings? When I first arrived at music school, a total stranger came up to me with a proposition. (It didn't take long for me to figure out that he was the Wind Ensemble Conductor.) He said that he could give me a brand-new bassoon, free bassoon lessons, and a full scholarship if I would agree to play in his ensemble! I already had a scholarship, so I wasn't very tempted by his peculiar offer. But it certainly taught me a lesson about supply and demand in the woodwind section.

THE BRASS FAMILY

Praise him with the sounding of the trumpet.   **Psalm 150:3**

Before we delve into the differences of each instrument, I want to remove a common misconception from your mind. When you think about the brasses, please do *not* just think of them only as *loud*. Some of the most beautiful sounds you will ever hear are quiet melodies on the horn or trumpet, even pianissimo passages from the trombones. Brass instruments are very versatile, and this extends to a wide spectrum of dynamic contrasts.

Perhaps this fortissimo caricature of brasses stems from the experiences of early students. When you first begin on a brass instrument, it's usually easier to play loudly than softly. But if parents can endure a while until better control is obtained, the results can be wonderful.

There are a few physical facts to consider before sending your little Michael out to the brass choir. Does he have braces on his teeth? It is very difficult to play a brass instrument wearing braces, and many instructors will refuse to accept him. In this case it would be wise to steer your child to another instrument, such as a violin, or a flute.

Another physical fact to note is the child's teeth, or rather, his "bite." Most people have an overbite, where the upper teeth extend out over the lower teeth. For brass playing, that is excellent. If your upper and lower teeth come together directly, that's fine. too. But if your child has an underbite, I don't recommend a brass instrument. It can be done, but they will have extra difficulties to overcome.

The trumpet. Like the flute in the woodwinds, the highest part of the brass choir goes to the preeminent trumpet. Also like the flute, the trumpet is *very* popular with children—ask any band director. Apparently kids want to be heard, and the trumpet assures this. Since trumpet melodies are quite prominent, it is a natural for confident, extroverted children.

At first some children will complain about its rather small cup-shaped mouthpiece. (French horn students make this same complaint about their small funnel-shaped mouthpieces.) But a good brass instructor can help almost all students overcome this obstacle and develop the proper embouchure control. The "embouchure" refers to the various muscles around the lips that are used when playing a wind instrument.

The French horn. The French horn (or just "horn") may not seem quite as flashy as the trumpet, but it can produce beautiful, soaring melodies. Ever since Beethoven used the valve horn in his Ninth Symphony, composers have written multitudes of romantic passages for the horn. Although not used as much in popular music, there could never be a full orchestra or a band without a complement of horns.

The horn can seem a bit reluctant to reward a child with melodic sounds at first. So much of horn playing is involved with mastering the tiny muscles of the embouchure that it takes a while to produce the desired results. This challenge also cuts down on the competition factor. But when you sit in an audience someday watching your Stephen play a Mozart Horn Concerto, you'll know that it was worth the wait.

The trombone. For many children the trombone is the easiest introduction to the brass instruments. It has a larger mouthpiece to work with, and its popularity among brasses is second only to the trumpet. Kids love to hear (and see) its long slide "glissando" from note to note, but this unique slide technique can make in-tune playing difficult at first.

Instead of simple valves to press or holes to cover, pitches from the trombone are produced by its slide—divided into seven positions. Although these are not visually marked, students are usually quick to get a feel for them. In an amazingly short time—often quicker than his friends on the trumpet or horn—the student trombonist is producing melodies.

The tuba. The lowest-pitched member of the brass family is the tuba. Despite the comical references sometimes associated with this instrument, the tuba can produce some marvelous music. Especially in the twentieth century, composers have finally learned to write more than "oompah-pah" music for tuba, and many band parts bring out the noble quality of this instrument.

Many tuba players also learn a number of auxiliary brass instruments such as the baritone or the sousaphone. Brass teachers are usually quick to teach students these and other "extra" instruments (such as cornets, euphoniums, sousa-phones, and flugelhorns) so that bands and brass ensembles have a wide variety of tone colors.

I should probably warn you about "spit valves." That's right, spit, or at least, "water." You see, while a brass instru-ment is being played, water slowly builds up within the tube, and sooner or later must be disposed of. Each instrument has a small valve in which the player (during a pause in the music) "blows out" his instrument. (Hopefully, he is not practicing on an expensive Oriental rug.) Brass players don't make a big deal out of this, and fortunately they are very discreet about this technique.

PERCUSSION

Praise him with the clash of cymbals.   **Psalm 150:5**

The world of percussion has changed a great deal in the latter part of the twentieth century, and it is a change for the better! In former days the percussion section was often the dungeon of the school band or orchestra—the place to send students who were too untalented to play a "real" instrument like a clarinet. They were relegated to hitting a cymbal or drum.

Mallet instruments. Thankfully, student percussionists have long since been liberated, and serious percussion has now been "put on the map." Much of this came through a marvelous emphasis on the fantastic (but challenging) *mallet* instruments such as the marimba, xylophone, and vibraphone. Now, instead of simply counting 183 measures of rest and then hitting a drum, percussion students play Bach sonatas transcribed for marimba! Suddenly, percussionists are taking themselves very seriously—and the rest of the music world is sitting up and taking notice!

These keyboard-like mallet instruments can play melodies, harmonies, solos, and accompaniments. Of course, they mostly play transcriptions, that is, music originally written for other instruments but now rearranged for xylophone, etc. With these new transcriptions, a whole new world has been opened up to them, including arrangements by Bach, Haydn, Mozart, and hundreds of other composers who died before these mallet instruments were ever dreamed of. Now student percussionists have some significant music to master.

I mention this in case your little Hank announces that he volunteered to be in the school percussion section, and you had your hopes set on seeing him play something else. Don't think of changing schools! Hank will be fine, and so will you. Percussion is *much* more than loudly beating drums. In fact, it can be quite fascinating.

The percussion world is quite unique. While violinists don't play cello and trombonists don't play the trumpet, the serious percussionist learns virtually *all* of the percussion instruments. Together with cymbals and drums (in great variety), there are the mallet instruments, bells, chimes, and a huge variety of "accessories" (triangles, tambourines, wood blocks, castanets, temple blocks, etc.).

Drums. Of course, the main percussion instrument in the standard orchestra is the timpani, or kettledrums. In a school or youth orchestra only the very best student gets to play the timpani. Indeed, he had better be good because if he makes a mistake everyone will certainly know about it!

Which brings up an important aspect of the percussionist. If you think that the first trumpeter's part is highly exposed in an ensemble, try being the timpanist. It takes more than good counting to wait for fifty-seven measures and suddenly come up fortissimo. It takes a great deal of confidence. There's simply no place to hide! You may want to consider this if your child doesn't like to stand out.

How do kids get hooked on percussion? A widespread approach is through the appeal of the drum set. You've seen thousands of them—from jazz trios to rock bands—and your child has see them too, perhaps with undisguised craving.

Whether you play in an orchestra, jazz band, or rock band, to become a truly great percussionist will take years of honing and perfecting technique. All percussionists will tell you that it takes work, expertise, sensitivity, and profound study.

Therefore, if your child Hank wants to play a drum set, don't run for cover. Instead, find a good, serious percussion teacher. Hank will build good drum set technique as well as be introduced to the important techniques of all the other percussion instruments. This could lead to many interesting possibilities; I have heard from professional classical percussionists who have taken this path. And if they continue to play on the drum set, a whole variety of possibilities could open up for them.

OTHER INSTRUMENTS

Praise him with the harp and lyre....

Psalm 150:3

Organ. Though we have already mentioned piano playing, there is still the organ as well as the harpsichord. Even in our day of ultra-specialization, performers on these instruments also play the piano, and many of them *started* on the piano. Only later did these students need special attention as required by the specific instrument.

Organists are often piano students who find that they have a natural talent and inclination for the instrument when they are needed to play the church organ. Soon, they will need an organ teacher who can work with them on the different techniques that this repertoire requires.

Harpsichord. In the same way, all harpsichordists are pianists or organists who got hooked on playing Baroque music. Thousands of people prefer to play (and hear) Bach's keyboard music on the harpsichord—as it was originally composed— than on its descendant, the piano. Nevertheless, a youth will need years of piano study and a specialized teacher before he or she will be ready to make such a shift to either the organ or the harpsichord.

Harp. The harp presents a unique situation. When you look at a harp, you may not realize that it is somewhat related to the piano keyboard. It uses both hands in creating chords and melodies, and some piano music can be played on the harp. Therefore, it should not surprise you that most harpists have previously studied piano.

Many students are attracted to the beauties of the harp and want to try it if an instrument is available. Usually harps belong to a school—they can cost thousands of dollars, and sets of strings can run into the hundreds—but harps can be rented or purchased (especially small "troubadour" harps for beginning students). It may be difficult to find a harp teacher, but the wonderful music it produces makes the extra effort worthwhile.

Studying harp is also a good way to find a unique place in the orchestra, where it has some splendid parts. As a classical guitarist—a fantastic instrument, but not one used in many orchestras—I always envied players of orchestral instruments. Learning that my college orchestra needed harpists, I found a good teacher, studied hard, and soon found myself in the midst of all my friends.

Guitar. As in the case of percussionists, guitarists often start in the world of popular music, then branch out to other styles. Whether the goal is to play a classical guitar concerto with the Philharmonic or to play an electric one in a band, I recommend that the young student begin with a *nylon*-string guitar.

Let's clear up some confusion about types of guitars. There are electric guitars and non-electric guitars. The former always use metal strings, but the latter come in two rather misnamed categories: those with nylon strings (usually called "classical" guitars or "folk" guitars), and those with metal strings (usually called "acoustic" guitars).

As you might imagine, nylon strings are much easier on the fingers than metal strings. Your daughter Anna has enough to work on and does not need the added discouragement of painful, irritated fingertips. Until Anna has been encouraged by some proficiency on the instrument (and her fingers have developed the needed callouses), save the metal strings for later.

There are, of course, dozens of diverse guitar styles one can learn. While I do not wish to pass judgment on them all, I do recommend that—regardless of style preferences—all guitarists learn to read music. Not only will this free them from the limited world of just "playing chords," it will enable them to play with many other instruments and broaden their musical experience.

When the great guitarist Christopher Parkening started playing guitar, the only guitarist he knew was his cousin, John Marshall. John gave him two pieces of excellent advice: "First, start with classical guitar—then you will have a good foundation in technique; second, get the recordings of Andrés Segovia. He's the greatest guitarist in the world." Parkening took this advice, and now he is another of the greatest guitarists of this century.

Again I stress, find a qualified teacher. Too many young guitarists learn only by picking up musical snatches from their peers. While this method can be helpful, bad habits spread quickly this way—habits which will definitely hurt them later as they try to master more difficult music.

By learning the guitar, your child will obtain skills that will allow him to learn other fretted strings: mandolin, banjo, electric bass guitar, etc. Almost all the players of these instruments began on the guitar and later branched out to their preferences. So if your child is determined to play banjo, it might be a good idea to try some guitar lessons first.

WHEN TO BEGIN?

Every child is unique, and everyone's circumstances are different. Obviously, there are practical considerations to weigh, such as "Is there a qualified teacher nearby?" and "Is the instrument available?" All instruments are not alike when it comes to the age of beginning study.

There are some general points to consider as well. A child who starts studying an instrument too early may be frustrated at his inability to produce satisfactory results. This may generate a negative experience that can be hard to erase in later years when the child could otherwise have been successful at music.

Nevertheless, encouraging children to begin *as soon as they are ready* will give them a head start in music and its beneficial by-products. Ultimately, the key question you must ask about your child (of any age) goes something like this:

"How earnestly does my child want to learn music?"

If he is excited about it and has a sincere desire to succeed, almost any obstacle can be overcome. If he has moderate interest, he may do fine for a while but later become discouraged. Obviously, if he doesn't want to learn, he won't. In this latter case, it might be best to wait until interest can be developed. Don't worry, it can come later, to everyone's benefit.

I am well aware of the many conflicting opinions on this subject. Different music teachers will give you different answers to the question, "What's the earliest age to start music lessons?" I know they will because I've asked dozens of them myself, and received dozens of different answers. The spectrum runs between the Suzuki philosophy (which starts children very early) and the classicists (which won't begin until years of prerequisites are obtained such as a great deal of concert-going and a strong music appreciation background). Rather than add one more opinion to the confusion, I'll give you a good rule of thumb:

> Talk to different teachers, find one you personally trust, and go with that teacher's opinion.

If you have met a good Suzuki teacher who is enthusiastic about starting your child at two years old, give it a try. If, on the other hand, the teacher you feel the most comfortable with says to wait, perhaps you had better wait.

In chapter 6, I will spend a lot of time discussing how a parent can recognize a good teacher from a bad one. In the meantime I will provide you a list of *very* general starting ages for different instrument groups. This is simply a guide, with many exceptions. Indeed, if you show it to any music teacher, you'll probably find places where he or she disagrees. But I hope it will help you in your consideration as you compare these ages to those of your own children.

EARLIEST AGES FOR MOST CHILDREN
TO BEGIN MUSIC STUDY

VOCAL (that is, *private vocal study*):
Girls: 12 to 14 years old
Boys: 15 to 16 years old

INSTRUMENTAL
Piano: 3 to 4 years old
Strings: 3 to 5 years old
Woodwinds: 8 to 10 years old
Brass: 9 to 11 years old
Percussion: 9 to 11 years old
Harp: 10 to 12 years old
Guitar: 8 to 10 years old

Making It Work for *You* — Try This:

1. First, find out how much your child knows about the different instruments and instrument groups. Ask questions about each. See if she can identify their sounds from recordings.

2. Get a book with pictures of all the different instruments. Go over each one with your child.

3. Ask questions that will help you discern if your child has a preference for one instrument group or one instrument in particular.

4. Do you know any musicians, even amateurs, who could demonstrate their instrument to you and your child?

5. Does your child have any peers who are already studying on an instrument? Which one, and why? Take your child to meet with them and see their instruments.

Interlude One:

For Parents
of Instrumentalists

♦ ♦ ♦

Having read the previous chapter, I'm certain you can see the wonderful advantages of learning an instrument. However, before your child can learn one, he or she has to *get* one! There are a lot of ways—some better than others—to get the right instrument. Furthermore, once your child has one, it is extremely important to take good care of it. Let's spend a little time on these very practical matters.

EASY ACCESS TO A GOOD INSTRUMENT

To begin with, to learn an instrument a child must have that instrument at his or her disposal. I am constantly bewildered by the number of parents who want their child to learn piano— even sending them to private lessons—when they don't even *own* a piano. As you might guess, this doesn't work very well.

Part of learning an instrument involves having free access to it at any given time of the day. If a student has even a few minutes free, he or she should be able to sit down with the instrument. Even if your child usually practices at the same hour every day, it's a good idea to encourage impromptu practice sessions when time allows.

Especially for children, the pride of personal ownership is extremely motivating. Even if the instrument is rented or borrowed from a school, kids need to feel a sense of ownership—"this is *my* instrument." As they advance, students get to know the unique quality of their instruments.

This was recently demonstrated in my family. After many months of leasing used violins, one of my sons was finally rewarded with a brand-new beautiful violin—his very own, which he had even helped to pay for. This sense of ownership produced an immediate and dramatic change in his attitude. Suddenly, he was the "star violinist" who wanted to play for every occasion and practice whenever possible. Considering some of our previous altercations at practice time, I consider this money to be the best I ever spent!

Some of you may be getting nervous about spending all this money on an instrument, especially if you don't have it to spend. Later in this chapter, I'll deal with this issue thoroughly and show you ways to get good instruments at good prices. But the principle remains: Your child needs the instrument at home. If you can't afford a piano, let your child play flute—it's much less expensive.

You wouldn't put your daughter Susan on a soccer team if she didn't own a soccer ball. You wouldn't send your son Jeff to the football game if he didn't have his own helmet and shoulder pads. With every successful endeavor, certain equipment is a prerequisite. The only exception to this involves very large instruments such as the harp, some percussion (tympani, etc.), and perhaps the organ. Two things must be arranged ahead of time for your child to have a good learning experience on one of these instruments.

First, find a school or church that owns the instrument Johnnie is studying and make arrangements for him to have access to that instrument as often as possible.

Second, find a similar substitute for home use. For example, if you don't have a full-size pedal harp, get a smaller "troubadour" harp for home. A drum "practice pad" is an excellent substitute for real kettle drums when practicing the necessary rhythms. If you don't happen to have a pipe organ in your home, your child can still work with a small electric organ or a piano. (If you *do* have a pipe organ in your home, I'm impressed!)

THE SCOURGE OF DILAPIDATED MUSICAL INSTRUMENTS

Some time ago one of my young sons brought home a recorder he had purchased from his school. Hearing him practice in his room made me seriously wonder if he had any musical talent at all. Realizing that he was discouraged, I stopped to help him—only to find that I sounded as awful on that recorder as he did. The instrument was a piece of junk! We both enjoyed ceremoniously placing it right where it belonged: in the garbage can.

There are few things more discouraging than trying to learn music on an inadequate instrument. Frankly, music is hard enough to learn without this extra burden. I am not implying that all children need a Stradivarius to begin their study, but at least they shouldn't have to fight the instrument to make it play.

Even a master musician sounds terrible on a terrible instrument. I have been in many homes where a child is having to learn piano on an instrument apparently not tuned this century. (The resulting discords will never teach the student to love *music*, though he may develop a great affinity for science fiction movies.) Sadly, many instruments from school programs are defective and in need of repair—or disposal.

The point is clear: If your child is to learn to play an instrument, he must begin with a decent instrument. Furthermore, it must be kept in good condition. If this seems obvious to you, good! You have apparently not visited some of the homes and schools I have. As we seek to turn our children on to the world of music, let's not give them the unfair disadvantage of an inadequate instrument.

You'll be glad to know that—once I found him a satisfactory instrument—my son was quite talented on the recorder!

FINDING A GOOD INSTRUMENT

If your son Rich wants to play the oboe, and finances are not a problem, purchasing an instrument is not much of a challenge. You simply tell your secretary to call all the music stores in town, find the very best oboe money can buy, and write out a check. Maybe if you pay enough, you can have it monogrammed with Rich's initials, gift wrapped, and delivered.

But most of us—who live with tight budgets and kids growing out of shoes almost hourly—don't fit this scenario.

So what should you do? Your son Tim wants to play the oboe, and you're barely getting your bills paid. You call the local music store and they want to sell you a new oboe for $4,000! You want the best for your child, but... there's no way!

Wait... maybe there is. Let's look at all the possibilities:

Using a school instrument. This idea may not work for everyone, since not all children go to public schools. But for the thousands who do, this is an excellent way to obtain an instrument without cost—in a way, though, you've already paid for it in your taxes!

Of course, not all the instruments are in mint condition, but many school systems possess some fine ones. The first thing to do is to talk as early in the school year as possible with the band or orchestra director. It is the director's job to know the condition of the school's instruments, and often he or she can repair a damaged one and restore it to playing condition.

Believe me, when music directors find out that you, as parents, are serious about your child's musical study, they will find you a good instrument somehow. Remember, they want their ensembles to sound great, so they are at least as interested as you are. A great-sounding band or orchestra has a lot to do with the director's job security!

Using a school instrument is the least expensive way to find out your child's immediate abilities. If Susie shows promise and enthusiasm on her instrument, sooner or later she will need one of her own.

Borrowing an instrument. Believe it or not, there are probably enough instruments sitting in the closets and attics of the homes in your city to outfit every would-be player in the country. Thousands and thousands of instruments are purchased every year, played for a while and then stored away, but seldom sold. Why not put them back to work?

Almost everyone knows someone—a friend, colleague, or relative—who has an instrument collecting dust in his house somewhere. Your boss' old clarinet he played in high school, your Uncle Peter's violin, a trumpet in your neighbor's garage... there are instruments out there, if you're willing to look for them. I have found that most people are delighted to have the instrument put to good use again.

Incidently, this might be a good place to mention the possibilities of bartering. Suppose you know someone who has an old violin that would be perfect for your Sam. Perhaps they might not want to give it away, but if Sam can work for it—giving them some service without wages—they would be willing for him to use the instrument.

Start asking around. Begin with family (even distant relatives), then try your neighbors and friends. Put up notices on neighborhood and church bulletin boards: "Wanted: a student flute for a child destined to become the world's greatest flutist." Give it a try—no cost is involved. The worst that can happen is that you'll meet some new friends.

Renting an instrument. Renting is a very viable option for acquiring an instrument. Some music stores allow the rental fees to accrue toward the eventual purchase of the instrument. The two basic suppliers of rental instruments are music stores and professional musicians.

With a music store you will have a larger selection, but the rental policies may be inflexible. Try to speak with the manager, not some clerk who has to "follow the rules" and can't bargain with you. Don't forget to ask about insurance; you want to know who pays for the instrument if it gets smashed to bits. Always call every music store for miles around, for prices can vary enormously. It may be well worth a long drive to find an instrument with a lower rental fee every month.

You may also want to ask around for private rentals from professional musicians and teachers in your area. If you don't know of any, call a local school music director, who should know the main teachers in your vicinity. You can even call the nearest symphony orchestra's office. Explain your situation to them; they are usually happy to put you in touch with an instrumentalist for the instrument you are looking for. Follow every lead you can find.

NOTE: Unless you are a musician yourself, you should have a musician you trust go with you to look at prospective rental instruments. This becomes even more important when buying! Over the years, I've helped to pick out dozens of instruments for friends and their children. Find someone who will look out for your best interests, or you may get stuck with a real lemon.

If you don't happen to have a musician for a friend, offer to pay one—it'll be worth the investment.

Buying a used instrument. Some people don't like to buy anything used. They prefer to start out with everything new—new cars, new houses, and new instruments. If you feel strongly about this, that's fine. Go to the next section. But buying a used instrument is a perfectly acceptable solution to your needs. There are very few hidden parts, and an experienced musician can tell a good instrument from a bad one in a matter of minutes.

Furthermore, many instruments—notably strings—actually increase in value and quality as they age. The very best brand-new violins aren't worth as much—nor do they sound as good—as an ancient Stradivarius. It's nice to own something that goes *up* in value over the years. This is an important factor to consider when reselling your instrument or trading it in to a music store when you're ready to upgrade to a better instrument. Unfortunately, this appreciation factor is not true for wind instruments, and particularly not for pianos. It simply depends on the instrument.

That is why it is very prudent to find an experienced musician to help you pick out a good instrument. If the sale is from a music store, they will often let you "test drive" the instrument for a few days. Take it directly to a good teacher for a critical evaluation. My wife's cello students sometimes bring her some very poor instruments. Her expertise has helped them avoid making such costly mistakes.

The best deals for used instruments are usually found not in the music store, but in the want ads of your local newspaper. This can be time consuming, but the savings can make it worthwhile, especially if you can find a musician to help in the evaluation. It only takes a few minutes for a musician to scan the paper for the best prospects, make a few calls, and settle on the best one or two possibilities for the two of you to visit.

Please don't assume that all cheap instruments from the want ads are junk. When my wife was a young girl in need of her first cello, her parents found an ad in the local paper. Two elderly ladies had an old cello in their attic, and happily sold it for fifty dollars. It was years later when my wife found out (through the need of a repair) that the instrument was actually worth thousands of dollars. She now uses this magnificent instrument professionally.

Buying a new instrument. Buying a new instrument is a bit like buying a new car; you don't want to hurry. There are always three things to keep in mind:

1. *Use a pro.* As I mentioned before, it is very helpful if a professional musician can help you pick out a new instrument. Probably this could be your child's teacher. I should mention that music teachers are generally not wealthy, and you should offer to pay whoever helps you pick out an instrument. If the musician declines such a fee, you might consider a small gift for him or her once the instrument has been selected.

2. *Shop around.* It is shocking to find the exact same flute selling for wildly fluctuating prices in different music stores. An instrument is too important an investment for you to simply walk into one store and buy the first one you find. Even if you live in a rural area with few music stores nearby, there are many companies making instruments that can be purchased through their catalogues. Always compare prices and purchasing options, using as many sources as possible.

3. *Take a "test drive."* In most situations you should be allowed to take an instrument home for a while to check it out thoroughly before deciding to purchase it. For good string instruments, some stores will let you "test drive" several

instruments for a week or so, to decide on your favorite. (Since this doesn't work well for pianos, you may be spending a lot of time in the piano store before an instrument is selected.)

Your child will be spending many, many hours with a new instrument—take the time needed to select the right one.

Congratulations! Now that you have this wonderful instrument, protect your investment by keeping it in good working order. Pianos must be tuned regularly, and all instruments should have a "check up" at least once a year. This doesn't have to be very formal or expensive. Have either your teacher or some other professional check it for problems that sometimes develop.

Celebrate the new instrument! When you get a new one (even if it's used, it's new to you!), have a special dinner or some other fun. And watch your child's interest in music soar!

Chapter Six

The World of Music Lessons

◆ ◆ ◆

"How can my child get the most out of music lessons?"

O f the hundreds of musicians I know and work with, very, very few would consider themselves self-taught. Even those rare individuals who possess an enormous amount of natural talent have also spent many years learning music from specific music teachers. The art of music is one that is "caught," and it is best caught from an inspiring teacher.

Of course, there are many forums in which music can be taught. Unlike most of a child's schooling, which is confined to a classroom situation, the wonderfully infectious love of music can be caught in a private lesson, a small ensemble, a classroom, a large orchestra—or simply in front of a CD player.

I have spent many hours in all of these forums—as the teacher, conductor, and (years ago) student—and each has its advantages and disadvantages. But if you truly want to interest your child in music, please consider the possibility of private lessons.

PRIVATE LESSONS?

Why private lessons? Why not have Billy learn tuba in a class-room as he learned algebra and grammar? Can't music be learned in a group setting?

Yes, some of it can. Many schools today offer excellent class-room courses taught by inspiring music educators with won-derful results. These are usually "general music" type classes and not tuba classes, but it is not impossible to teach instru-ments in a group setting. I've done it many times.

Nevertheless, it is unthinkable for a talented instrumentalist to have only classroom instruction without private lessons; this could be detrimental to his ongoing musical progress.

Over the past few centuries, instrumental techniques have become more and more intricate and specialized. The tradi-tions of teaching the various instruments have been handed down and refined from generation to generation. Hundreds of critical factors are involved, from the best arm positions to the proper way of sitting while playing an instrument. Today, it is virtually impossible for the same music teacher to excellently teach both violin and trumpet, except at the most rudimentary levels.

This is a somewhat controversial point. Every year, music schools send out thousands of fine music teachers who are trained to teach many different instruments. But it must be pointed out that these teachers, even the best ones, can only teach all these instruments at a very basic level. As soon as a tal-ented child advances past the beginning stage of learning, the non-specialized teacher—understandably only able to teach highly technical skills on his primary instrument—often can be a hindrance to the child's progress.

And, of course, in a classroom or ensemble setting, even the greatest teachers are limited by time and space. If a teacher has a group of twelve violins, four violas, five cellos, and two double basses, how much time can she possibly spend with each child? Suppose your child Lucy is playing third viola. Can the teacher even notice that she is slipping into the bad habit of, say, holding her bow too tightly? And yet, without such correction Lucy's technique will be seriously impeded.

I recently asked my friend James Kraft, trombonist in the National Symphony, about his early musical training. Like many wind players, he began playing in his elementary school band. Yet he insisted that the reason his early training was effective was that his band conductor *required* each student to take private lessons and to practice one hour every day. It goes without saying that this band sounded *very* good!

PRIVATE LESSONS SOON!

As I wrote this paragraph, my wife finished giving a weekly cello lesson to a fairly new student. This young cellist is now in the tenth grade, but started on the instrument in her school program in the fourth grade. Her school music teacher, a violinist, was an inspiring "starter" who taught string classes. After a year or so of these mixed groups, this student should have been sent to a private cello teacher to continue her advanced skills.

Instead, she spent six years without effective supervision, and learned six years of bad habits that simply cannot be broken. Like a garden that has not been properly tended, her technique is full of weeds. For her to progress as a cellist, she would have to unlearn many of these habits, and she is now so far behind the other cellists of her age (each with years of private lessons) that her future as a musician has been critically jeopardized.

I'm afraid this is all too common. Private teachers cringe when they are approached by new students who have spent years playing in school programs without the supervision of a specialized teacher. There is always so much to unlearn, so many bad habits to try and conquer. Many times, this process is so arduous that the students become discouraged and give up. What an unnecessary waste of talent.

Why not learn the good habits to begin with? They are really no more difficult or time consuming than the bad ones students will develop without close supervision. But to consistently learn correct habits in instrumental playing, a private teacher is an absolute necessity. There are no exceptions.

This is certainly not a complaint against the thousands of dedicated music educators in our school system. It is simply that no one teacher can do everything, be everywhere in the class simultaneously, and see everything that every student is playing. It can't be done. It takes individual teaching and observation.

The most convincing evidence of this is to observe a good private teacher giving a lesson. He is not only listening intently, but vigilantly watching the student's every move. You will hear comments like:

"Your third finger is collapsing in this passage."
"Try this different fingering here."
"Your left arm is becoming too tense."

Can any classroom teacher constantly see and point out such miniscule—but crucial—factors to mastering an instrument? Of course not; it takes a private teacher to master music on any instrument.

Teaching music is not a standard formula that works the same way for every child because each student is unique. Some need super-encouragement, others a kick in the pants. A good private teacher, like a good doctor, will first analyze the student's whole situation and adapt the instruction to the needs of that specific child.

The ultimate argument for private lessons is, of course, the results. Of the thousands of musicians I know personally, I have never met even one professional performer—in any professional orchestra, chamber ensemble, or opera company—who has not had years of private instruction. They all have, and they will all tell you that private lessons are absolutely essential. Without exception!

FINDING THE RIGHT TEACHER FOR YOUR CHILD

I wish more parents would consider the long-term importance of this subject. A child's first private teacher has an inestimable impact on the future of how he will view music. The wrong teacher at this critical early stage can single-handedly rub out a lifetime of joyful music-loving. But the right teacher can have such a meaningful influence that it is never forgotten.

This was brought home to me when I recently asked James Buswell, a concert violinist and professor at the New England Conservatory of Music, about the teachers that have made a profound impression on his life. Even though Buswell had studied with some of the greatest string masters of our century, such as Ivan Galamian, he immediately began lauding his original teacher, a woman named Mary Canberg. "She was the one who first lit a fire under me," says Buswell, setting him on a road that has touched thousands with the love of great music.

But how do we find such a Mary Canberg for our children? There is no one simple answer, but there are many important principles that you should keep in mind during your search.

1. *Do not simply go to the first one you find.* Take some time to look for the right one, just as you would buy a house or a car. A private teacher may not cost as much as a house (I hope!), but his or her combined years of teaching and expertise are crucial for the proper development of your child's musical skills. It's worth a bit of searching.

2. *Ask the opinion of other parents of musical children.* What experience, good or bad, have they had with different teachers? How well do their children appreciate their teachers?

3. *Ask the opinion of other musicians you may know* as well as music teachers at school. It's their business to know the qualified teachers in your area.

4. *Keep in mind that the best musical performers are not always the best music teachers.* Often I hear of a mother who insists, "My child must study with someone who plays in the local professional orchestra." Certainly, our orchestras contain many good teachers as well as good performers, but the two professions are not synonymous. Never overlook a instructor (who might be a tremendous teacher) just because he doesn't have a full-time performing job. Some of the finest ones teach so well and so often that there is little time left to perform.

5. *Consider a teacher's reputation above his or her professional associations.* Years ago, I might have insisted you check with such organizations as your local music union, or the Music Teachers National Association. These are certainly worthy groups to contact, but don't be limited by them in your choice. Many of the finest teachers in the country do not belong to such organizations. Their reputations are enough to recommend them.

6. *Try to find a music teacher who holds a degree in music.* I suppose it's theoretically possible for a gifted teacher to have never been to music school, but it's rather unlikely. The teacher's degree may be in music performance, music education, or various other music programs.

7. *Talk at length to a prospective music teacher.* Find out about the teacher's educational philosophy. He may be a disciple of such methods as Suzuki, Kodaly, Dalcrose, or Orff, or may have his own techniques. All methods have merit, but

the most significant factors are the skill and the enthusiasm of the teacher.

8. *Talk to the teacher about the objectives and goals he has for his students.* Does he give assignments each week? Does he endeavor to teach students *how* to practice? (More about this in the next chapter, "Practicing.")

9. *Talk to the teacher about your child's specific temperament, interests, and practice habits.* Do you sense a sensitivity to the individual needs and characteristics of different children? Do you sense a profound enthusiasm for teaching?

10. *Find out how often he requires his students to perform.* Do *not* even consider a teacher who does not require performing at all. I will explain the benefits of performing in chapter nine.

11. *If possible, attend a recital of the teacher's students.* There is nothing better to recommend a teacher than the fruit of his efforts.

12. *Make sure you completely understand all of the teacher's practical policies:* manner of payment (each week, each month, each semester), arrangements for making up missed lessons due to sickness, inclement weather, etc.

Always keep in mind that you are not looking for the world's greatest teacher, but the right teacher for *your* child. It may take a while, but it will be worth the extra effort.

Of course, sometimes you stumble upon the best teacher with amazingly little effort. Opera singer Myra Merritt found her first teacher in the Yellow Pages, and he was fantastic for her. Jerome Hines went to his first teacher for the simple reason that this was the teacher his next-door neighbor used!

My favorite "best teacher" story comes from the master guitarist Christopher Parkening. When his talent began to show, his parents called the local music store for a teacher. They were told that the guitar teacher's schedule was completely filled, but the teacher knew of a family from Spain that had recently moved into town and whose father and three sons played guitar. This new family turned out to be none other than the Romeros, the "royal family" of the guitar. Soon Parkening was studying with the father, Celedonio Romero, and his son Pepé, and spent four years learning from this incredibly talented family.

Let's end this section with an amusing story about what you *don't* want in a private teacher. Remember those zany comedians the Marx Brothers? Chico Marx, the hilarious pianist of the group, took piano lessons as a boy from a teacher with a rather weird limitation. She taught just the right hand (and only "faked it" with the left when she played). If Chico asked what to do with his left hand, the teacher whacked his right knuckles with a ruler, shrieking, "Never mind—*that* hand is where the music is!"

He became one of the best one-handed piano players in New York.

But don't you think that your child deserves a little better than the teacher Chico had?

COSTS, TRAVEL, TIME, AND OTHER PRACTICAL ITEMS

How much should you spend on lessons? If I suggest a dollar amount, this book will immediately be outdated, since prices go up every year. (Music teachers are entitled to cost-of-living raises, too, aren't they?) It is best to check around in your area until you find the overall amount that most teachers are charging for that instrument. Be suspicious of teachers who charge a great deal too much or too little.

Even if your finances are very tight, do not try to bargain with the teacher's rates. Bargaining is for yard sales and flea markets, not music lessons. If you can't afford it, don't go to that teacher. The only exception might be if you both agree to a bartering situation—that is, if you have a service or skill you can offer the teacher in return. Even then, be aware that awkward situations may result.

Speaking of costs, I must put in a plea for the music teachers of the world: pay your bills on time, *every time!* It is appalling how many teachers are abused in this way. Professional music teachers make their living this way, and if a number of people "forget the check this week," it can seriously limit their activities (like eating!).

In the world of music lessons, it is common practice for the student to go to the teacher, rather than the other way around. This is standard teaching policy and should be respected. I am often amused (and a little shocked) by those parents who seem to think it is too far to travel a few blocks to the music teacher. I have known students who travel weekly from Washington, D.C. to New York City for a good music teacher!

An interesting story to illustrate this policy happened in Washington during the Carter administration. There is a gifted violin teacher in the Virginia suburbs who was recommended to the President as an instructor for his daughter, Amy. This teacher was honored with an invitation to come to the White House every week to teach the first daughter. But the teacher stuck to her policy, and I don't blame her. The President was politely informed that all her students must come to her studio. So Amy (with her Secret Service agents) made the trip each week thereafter.

While we're on the subjects of travel and cost, I want to mention the option of studying privately with a teacher in a music store or music school. This may be the best alternative for some, and certainly many stores and schools offer the services of excellent teachers. Nevertheless, select each teacher yourself, just as you would select someone teaching out of his or her home. Never assume that those who work at a particular institution are all impeccably qualified. They may be, but be sure to check out the one who instructs your child. You should also realize your cost for these teachers will generally be higher since the institution usually takes a portion of your check for its overhead.

If you live in or near a large city (or a university with a music department), you have a few more possibilities. Many music schools offer preparatory music programs for young students. Furthermore, they all have music teachers who take private students on the side. As we shall discuss in chapter eight, an extra advantage here is the possibility of playing in these schools' orchestras and ensembles.

TIME: THE HIDDEN COST OF MUSICIANSHIP

TIME! Perhaps the more difficult "price" in private lessons is the price of time. This includes *your* time (the time needed for you to transport your child to and from lessons and rehearsals), as well as the student's time. Many young students take lessons that are 1/2 hour long, while older students take hour lessons.

A parent needs to count the cost when a child begins any new activity, including music lessons. We have an expression that easily applies to time management of children: You can't add something without subtracting something. Unless your child is remarkably bored before the lessons begin, you may need to subtract something from his schedule. Which brings up the next topic.

TIME PRESSURE ON YOUR CHILDREN!

A word of caution: Help your children to find a balance with their many activities. When I see some young students with music lessons, sports, church activities, and intense academic pressures, I become very concerned about their well-being.

As much as we want the best for our children, we can't give them all the best at the same time. Children are not adults. They are simply not equipped to deal with all the time pressures of such a busy schedule. Every child is different—what can be easily handled by one will utterly crush another. So let's be sensitive to how much we give our kids at the same time. We want them to encounter a wide variety of experiences, but we don't want to overwhelm them!

HOW TO SUPPORT THE TEACHER

Once you have found a music teacher who seems right for your child, there is still some preparation to do. To begin with, your first job is to minimize the apprehension associated with that first lesson. The child should have already met the teacher, if at all possible, but even so Joey may still need reassurance and encouragement. Do all you can to have this first lesson be a special day, perhaps following the lesson with a trip to the ice cream store.

Some parents desire to sit in on each lesson. This may be reasonable at first, to make sure that all three parties—teacher, student, and parent—are working well together toward the mutual goal. Some teachers actually prefer this, so that the parent can help the student during his practice sections.

Nevertheless, sitting in is not recommended as an ongoing practice. It can inhibit the teacher and give the child a confused feeling of divided authority. Most instructors are uncomfortable with it, and many refuse to consider it.

Instead, show your child that you have complete trust and confidence in his teacher. Always speak very highly of him or her when talking to your child, and treat the teacher with absolute respect and courtesy in the child's presence. For the lessons to have the best effect, your child should feel that *you* are extremely grateful to have such a fine instructor.

Parents should maintain open and honest communication with the teacher. One of the best things to ask is, "How can I help to see that my child practices properly?" Most teachers, delighted at such a helpful question, will give you a variety of great ideas.

It is not enough for a parent to simply enforce practice times. Especially for young students, parents should be involved enough to make certain that the child is not wasting practice time.

If a disagreement should ever come between you and the teacher, *NEVER* debate it in front of your child. Work this out privately as two adults, perhaps on the phone or at a specially requested appointment. Never discuss such disagreements with the child. If the student senses that his teacher and parent are in a quarrel, his respect for *both* of them may be lowered—to his educational detriment.

There are a number of practical ways you can help the teacher. One of the most important ways is your promptness in arriving for each lesson. It is imperative that the child show up on time: Teachers often schedule their students at set intervals (such as 5:30, 6:30, 7:30, 8:30—I know teachers with over fifty scheduled private lessons each week!). If you show up fifteen minutes late for your 5:30 lesson, it can affect many others.

Obviously, if you show up late, even for the best of reasons, do not ask or expect the teacher to give your child a full lesson. I'm afraid you'll have to assume the loss. Otherwise, it will throw off everyone's lesson who follows yours!

With rare exceptions (such as a sudden illness or other unforeseeable emergency), your child's weekly lessons should be a high priority in your schedule. Be considerate of the teacher's time and don't call shortly before a scheduled lesson and say that your child "can't make it this week." Many teachers, like doctors or dentists, make it a policy that unless you call at least twenty-four hours in advance, you must pay for all cancelled lessons. They don't like to do this, but they have to have order, as well as a regular income. (Like any other person with a family budget, they need to know beforehand exactly what they will earn each month.)

Parents don't enjoy paying for missed lessons, either, so this situation is best avoided by careful planning. If you know that your child will be unable to make a lesson, give the teacher as much advance notice as possible. Hopefully, a special make-up lesson can be arranged.

Ultimately, the best support you can give the teacher is to remind him that you appreciate his work (little Christmas gifts are great!) and that you will do whatever is necessary to help him successfully instruct your child. Teachers deeply cherish such parents. And in this happy atmosphere, guess who benefits the most? That's right, your child.

Making It Work for *You* —Try This:

1. Call several other parents you know whose children take private lessons. What are their experiences?

2. Find out what teachers in your area give lessons on the instrument you want your child to learn. Talk to at least two of them about the items covered in this chapter.

3. Work out a weekly schedule for you and your child that includes the lesson and practice time needed.

4. Once you have selected the right teacher for your child, sit down to consider ways in which you can help or encourage this very special person.

Chapter Seven

In Search of the Lost Chord: Practicing

◆ ◆ ◆

"How can I motivate my child to love practicing?"

I know that some parent is out there—one who has sometimes had to enforce practicing with a loaded shotgun—who, after reading the above question, may wonder if I have lost my mind. *LOVE practicing?! He must be joking. Don't all kids hate practicing?!*

No.

As a matter of fact, many kids love to practice. They can't wait to spend hours alone with their instrument, honing their skills and reveling in the joy of playing music.

Are these weird kids? No, they're perfectly normal, healthy, happy, well-adjusted, fun-loving children. They just happen to be infected with a tremendous love of music.

Since I was rather a late-bloomer in music, I can't speak much of my own practicing experience as a young child. But my wife is an excellent example. Throughout much of elementary school and all of high school, every morning she set her alarm an hour earlier than needed, so that she could practice her cello before school, as well as afterward.

Her teacher didn't ask her to. Her parents didn't require it.

No one did. She did it because *she* wanted to practice. And there are many fine students just like her.

However, not all parents are that fortunate. Not every young student loves to practice. You already knew that, didn't you? Otherwise, you wouldn't be reading this chapter!

What can be done to solve this problem that plagues many aspiring young musicians? How can a student who hates to practice be somehow transformed into a student who loves to practice? A good start in answering these questions is to examine the typical causes of practice-hating.

Let's make a list of some common reasons for this problem. Some of these problem areas can usually be resolved by the teacher, but many directly involve the parent. Either way, the parents and teacher need to work together on each particular obstacle.

As you observe the student, ask the following questions:

1. *Has the student ever been taught how to practice?* Is he left adrift, without assistance, not knowing how to best use his practice time or how to help himself improve?

2. *Is the student required to play only music he does not like?* This might include works of inferior musical caliber, "all études and no real pieces," or disagreements about musical styles.

3. *Is the music to be practiced appropriate for the student's level?* Is it too easy (boring) or too difficult (frustrating)?

4. *Consider practical factors.* Does the student have an adequate place where he or she can practice? And is the instrument decent, or is it in need of maintenance, repair, or replacement?

5. *Consider other distractions.* For example, must the student practice most often while siblings and friends have free playtime?

6. *Is the student being asked to practice more than is appropriate for his age level?* Are the student's practice sessions too long?

If I didn't get to everyone's situation in the first six problems, I'm sure number seven will hit home with all of us:

7. *Does the student need to develop some essential character qualities such as perseverance, diligence, and self-discipline?* If this last question sets off bells in your head, take heart and read on!

NO SUBSTITUTE FOR GOOD OL' HARD WORK

Whether you are a beginning student or are on your way to becoming an accomplished musician, there is a part of the growth process for which there is no substitute: *hard work.* This is not too popular with many kids—or many adults, for that matter. Everyone wants the end result—to play like a pro—but few are willing to put in the time and effort necessary to arrive there.

When I perform as a classical guitarist, it is quite common for someone in the crowd to later say, "I'd do anything to be able to play like you!" Although I usually smile and thank them, I always want to tell them, "No, you wouldn't."

Most people are unaware of how much time, effort, and expense it takes to train a professional performer. We live in a fast-paced society, and we are not used to waiting for results. Learning to skillfully play music will always take time—years of patience, sacrifice, and hard work.

One of my favorite verses, Proverbs 13:4, reads, "the desires of *the diligent* are fully satisfied." Musically speaking, the converse is also true: "If you are not diligent in your practicing, your desire to play well will never be realized." There are no shortcuts.

This is not to say that becoming a great musician is only a matter of practicing hard enough, long enough. There is a measure of *inborn talent* that cannot be taught, as anyone who has ever worked with world-class musicians will tell you. While recently conducting an opera with several top Met singers, I found myself pondering, "What could be so ridiculous as to think that I could sing as well as they, if I only worked as hard as they did and had the same teachers? Forget it!"

No, one cannot do without some God-given talent. It is the *combination* of both talent and dedication that produces the wonderful results for which everyone is looking. Since this book can't give your child any inborn talent—you'd better talk to God about that—perhaps it can help you in spurring them to work hard with the talents he *has* given them.

Let's look at some solutions to the seven common practice problems I mentioned earlier.

TEACHING STUDENTS *HOW* TO PRACTICE

This is primarily the responsibility of the teacher, but there are many aspects of this important subject that affect the parents. To begin with, parents should talk with the teacher about how they can encourage correct practicing.

It is not enough to merely enforce the piano practice time of your little Andy. At times you'll need to help him directly. "But I'm not a pianist!" you protest. Perhaps not. But you're not a scientist either, yet you help Andy with his science homework. You don't have to be an expert to require the work be done, encourage him when his spirits lag, and put in your own two cents worth of ideas as well. With some helpful advice from an experienced teacher, an involved parent can spot bad practice habits from the very beginning. This will benefit the child immensely.

For the sake of the student and the parent, the teacher should give definite assignments each week, preferably in writing. The student should know what his goals are for the week.

As he progresses as a student, he needs to know why he is practicing these particular pieces. Is it to learn rhythm or perhaps phrasing—or more proper technique? Practice will have meaning—and be much less painful—if the student can answer the question, "*Why* am I doing this?"

Even as a beginner, the child should begin learning the following important approach to practicing music:

1. Have a goal before starting.
2. Attempt the goal.
3. Critique the attempt.
4. Try again, striving to improve each time.

This is how music is learned. This is how beginners gradually become masters. Ultimately, it is here—in the practice time, not in the lessons themselves—that the critical improvement process truly takes place. After all, the lesson is only an hour or so each week. The practicing in between lessons takes many more hours. *This* is where the refinement occurs.

Cellist Anne Martindale Williams said it perfectly. She endeavors to teach her students "how to teach themselves."

In most accomplishments, the road from novice to master is one on which the individual learns to gradually become his own teacher or coach. This is, of course, a long process, but it is best started at the outset. The child should be taught to think and analyze, going from problem to solution.

For example, students need to learn the art of "divide and conquer." When they are overwhelmed by the task of learning a large composition, they must learn to divide it into parts, work on each segment individually, and then put the parts all together. *Slow* practicing is *so* important, so that the mind can carefully look at every aspect of the music, "putting it under the microscope." But it can be *so* hard for impatient little hands and minds.

This is where the parent comes in. Even the most musically untrained monitor can say, "Try that again, slowly." If you encourage them to do what they need to be doing, they will soon train themselves to do it. And then, almost anything can be accomplished.

As parents, our sensitivity to our children is essential in such matters. For instance, we need to know our children well so that we will sense when to intervene and when to "lay back" so the child discovers the learning process for himself.

Ultimately, the student must become his own teacher, asking *himself* the right questions to promote improvement. Christopher Parkening told me that he has a little sign on the music stand in his practice room. It reads, "Chris, what are you here for?" This reminds him of his *ultimate* purpose, to pursue excellence on his instrument so that he might glorify the Lord with his life and with the music that he plays.

GETTING KIDS TO PRACTICE MUSIC THEY HATE

Doesn't sound like much fun, does it? Yet much of the necessary skill needed to master any instrument comes as a result of repeatedly practicing exercises that are not pleasurable. Billy may dislike them, but they are essential to his musical growth (sort of like booster shots).

In addition, mastering an instrument requires that the student learn that instrument's repertoire. Many different pieces need to be studied but to be frank, some are greater masterpieces than others. Your child may love the music he played last month but detest the piece he has to work on this month.

And, of course, everyone's tastes are different. A work that is a favorite of the teacher may seem awful to the student. But the student has not yet progressed enough to know which pieces he should select. The teacher still needs to retain this control in order to instruct effectively. Again, at times the student needs to play music he doesn't especially like.

What can a parent do? There are three principle ways a parent might help in these situations:

1. *Talk to the teacher about the situation.* This presupposes some sensitivity on the part of the parent. I am *not* suggesting that the parent *complain* to the teacher. But good communication between parent and teacher is indispensable. Students often don't express themselves openly to the teacher, who may have no idea that the music is not enjoyed. Sometimes changes can be made; but if the teacher insists on keeping the same music, support him fully—and go on to ideas number two and three.

2. *Provide some additional pieces that he does enjoy* (or ask the teacher to do so). If a teacher assigns a lot of pieces which are not enjoyable, but essential, perhaps an extra work—a little "dessert"—could be added to keep up the student's spirits. Such an extra piece might even be selected by the student himself (with some guidance, as needed). This will increase the motivation level immensely.

3. *Help and encourage the child to endure this period of drudgery.* If no other music can be substituted or added, your responsibility is to help the student grin and bear it. This is *not* accomplished by lecturing! Avoid cold toughness—the student will resent both you *and* the music.

Instead, use your adult brain to point out interesting things in the music that the child does not grasp. If you are not a musician, ask your child's teacher for help. For instance, in fingering exercises, help him to overlook the strange sounds that may occur and concentrate on the fascinating finger work that is produced. Emphasize the benefits that will follow such efforts. Mention analogies with sports, how all athletes must undergo hours of grueling exercises to be ready to play at their best.

Finally, remember that there is a place for rewards. For a young child such a reward system could be as simple as a wall chart that gets a star for each exercise completed. I have known parents who successfully reward their children with everything from food to money. Use your imagination! Let your positive attitude influence them to be positive through the tough times.

EASY (BORING) MUSIC VS. DIFFICULT (FRUSTRATING) MUSIC

If a child isn't motivated about his music, it may be because he doesn't like the music—but, it could also be because the music is not at his level of technical proficiency.

Obviously, the teacher chooses the music, so this problem does not occur very often. But, occasionally, the teacher may select pieces that seem either too easy or too difficult in order to help a student develop musically or technically. You'll usually know when this is happening by the whining and complaining from your child that ensues.

Here are some ideas to help the student:

1. *If the music seems too easy, find ways make it more challenging.* Encourage the student to use the music as a technical exercise. After each phrase he should ask himself such questions as, "Was that good? How could it be better? How was the **tone** (is a beautiful sound being produced)? The **intonation** (are the different notes in tune with one another)? The **phrasing** (are the different phrases of music connected together well)? How about my fingers and my body position? Are they correct?"

"Easy" music is an excellent time to work on using a metronome. This device not only teaches good rhythm but is also essential for total control of the music. Only after the student has learned precision and control is he free for musical expression.

Make it fun for the young student. Play musical games with scales and arpeggios—which, incidentally, are the basic building blocks for every melody your child will ever play. When a young violinist says, "These scales are so boring," make him finish slowly, then give him a challenge. "Try the same scale two octaves higher, tremolo, with one foot in the air." As ridiculous as it looks (and sounds), they will *always* try, to everyone's amusement. The strained atmosphere vanishes in frivolity, and more work can now be done.

2. *If the music seems too difficult, find ways make it easier.* The most effective way to help a student who is overwhelmed with the difficult music before him is to help him "divide and conquer."

As I mentioned earlier, almost any composition can be learned *one step at a time.* The key to keeping a student motivated while learning a long, demanding work is to master it in small, conquerable sections.

Most students blanch at a difficult composition because of the sheer immensity of it. Tell them not to try and learn it all at once. Help them divide up the practice week: day one, the first eight measures; day two, the next eight; day three, putting them together, and so on. Remember the old proverb: "How do you eat an elephant? *One bite at a time!*"

To give variety, especially if several succeeding sections are each particularly difficult, sometimes change the order of sections in practice time. Whatever you do, create a positive attitude that says to the child, "Of course you can do it! Just take it one step at a time."

WHERE TO PRACTICE?

Many parents have little idea of how problematic this question really is. Especially if their child is a pianist, they respond, "Where should you practice? There's the piano! Go practice!" They may not even notice that their piano is in the middle of the family room, the main thoroughfare and living area in the house. At practice time, it may contain various noisy siblings (watching TV, playing, fighting) or dogs, cats, and snakes—not to mention a constant stream of people coming and going.

You'd have to be blind and deaf to practice in some places where kids are told, "Go practice!"

Where is a good place to practice?

Well, Mendelssohn's dad built his son extra rooms to help in his practicing. If you're as rich as Mendelssohn's dad was, this is a great idea. But the rest of us have to work something out within the present available space.

The two primary things needed in terms of location are:

1. A place that is quiet.
2. A place that is free from distractions.

Both of these assume a degree of isolation. For quality practicing, your child should be isolated from other sounds and from various distractions. Such distractions can include the commotion of moving people or pets, temptations such as TV or video games, or even poor lighting, heating, cooling, or ventilation.

To practice and learn, one needs to be able to concentrate on the task at hand. The best practice rooms have only one door so that they do not become thoroughfares of traffic. Windows are great for fresh air unless they look out over a baseball field or playground. Telephones in practice rooms are too distracting; let someone who is not practicing answer the phone.

If possible, the room should be in some out-of-the-way part of the house where the sounds from within and without do not disturb each other. Although you certainly don't have to have a designated "music room," it is helpful if all the musical supplies (instrument, music stand, metronome, etc.) are kept in the practice room.

It is preferable to have the *same* location for every day's practice. If a student is constantly bumped from one room to another, he does not feel settled, and his practice may also become inconsistent. Other children should be instructed that no one is to interrupt the child who is practicing.

As I alluded to above, the piano, since it is not very movable, poses a particular problem. Hopefully, your piano is not in the same room as your TV; they don't blend very well. Nevertheless, if the piano is not going to be in an isolated room, then scheduling practice times strategically is very critical. Let's now look closer at that entire issue.

WHEN TO PRACTICE?

Two children, Phil and Elizabeth, leave their weekly double bass lessons after being dutifully admonished to practice a good deal on this week's assignments. By the next lesson Phil has practiced four hours, while Elizabeth has only put in three and one-half hours. Which do you think will do better at the lesson? Phil, right?

Not this time. You see, Elizabeth faithfully practiced one-half hour each day that week. Phil neglected his instrument until the last day, when he attempted to cram his assignment into four hours. (Of course, this was obvious to his teacher.)

Cramming may (or may not) work for academic exams. It never works for music.

The key word is: *consistency*.

It is far more important that your child practice every day than to occasionally play his instrument all day long! Every time a student practices, he should be building on what he learned yesterday. Even the necessary muscular development can only take place with regular, uniform workouts.

Practice sessions can be compared to a bottle of vitamins. Would you go a week without vitamins and then swallow the entire bottle? I don't recommend it.

An interesting scripture is found in 2 Chronicles 30:22: "The Levites and priests sang to the Lord *every day*, accompanied by the Lord's instruments of praise." Even Temple musicians had to practice, and they did so consistently.

This concept should also be applied to the time allotted for practicing. It is very beneficial to have children practice at the same time each day. If you try to just "find the time," you never will. Practicing should become an integral part of their daily routine, with a definite time to start and finish.

In this way children know what is expected of them. There is less cause for argument, and you will both reap the benefits. When the session is over, never—unless the child obviously wants to continue—suggest that even more would be preferable. Let them be content with a good session; no guilt trips.

And *never, ever* use practicing as a punishment. "Just for that, young lady, you're going to practice an extra hour today!" This compels the child to view playing music in an extremely negative manner. We want them always to behold music in a positive light. Practicing can be hard enough work without having it forced upon a child for nonmusical reasons.

Practicing sometimes may have to occur while other siblings or friends are having a great deal of fun. Nonetheless, sensitive parents should consider scheduling practice times when such comparisons are not blatantly in the child's view. To insist on a practice time that coincides with the child's favorite activity is to invite resentment, or worse.

If you have more than one child taking lessons (not all on the piano), perhaps they can practice during the same time period. Then no one is envious of the other's activities, and all the practicing is done for the entire family. Everyone's schedule is simplified.

Three of our boys practice at the same time before school each morning, in three different rooms, with the doors closed. It works perfectly into the family schedule and prevents arguments about "what the other guys are getting to do." Of course, if you walk through the hall, the combined (yet musically unrelated) sounds of violin, cello, and piano can sound like an airplane crash. Actually, we love it; it sounds like our own little music school.

HOW LONG TO PRACTICE?

Such a question demands individual answers. It does not depend solely on such factors as the age and proficiency of the child. It should also take into account the child's personality, as well as his measure of the character qualities we will discuss in the next section.

Certainly, the teacher should suggest the initial amount of time that he deems appropriate, and this should be followed and monitored. Believe me, the first time that you hear complaints from your child about "all this practicing" should not send you a signal to shorten the time!

A good anecdote to tell your children is one recounted by Christopher Parkening, who studied with the renowned guitarist Andrés Segovia:

I once asked Segovia how many hours a day he practiced. He responded, "Christopher, I practice 2 1/2 hours in the morning and 2 1/2 hours every afternoon." I thought to myself, *If Segovia needs to practice five hours a day, how much more do I need to practice?*

Sometimes, especially for younger students, making a simple time chart is helpful. You may want to establish a system of rewards, as needed. Make it worth their while. Help them to see the principle of consequences in their practice: "What you sow, so shall you reap." A little practice reaps only a little progress, while greater practicing reaps greater progress.

Another argument to avoid is the one your child Monica may use on the day of a performance. "I don't need to practice," she confidently retorts. "I'll be playing my horn all evening in the concert." Sorry, Monica, but practicing and performing are two very different components of music. It doesn't work to try to substitute one for the other.

Trombonist James Kraft of the National Symphony has an excellent analogy for this situation, which should be shared with every young musician. He explains that, "practicing is like putting money *into* the bank. Performing is like taking money *out* of your bank account." Obviously, you can only take out as much as you have put into this musical bank account.

Although consistency is the basic principle in practicing, for many children it might be a good idea to have a day off once each week—a kind of "Sabbath rest." Obviously, if they *want* to practice on this day, I wouldn't stop them. But most of us need a break once in a while, and this day-off idea works very well for many children.

Of course, the parent and teacher need to communicate about this subject. As the teacher is the expert on music, so the parent is the expert on his or her child. If, after weeks of practicing and whimpering, you feel that this is too much for your child, you should confer privately with the teacher. The same is true if you sense that your child is not being sufficiently challenged in his practice time.

How does a parent sense that his child is being over- or under-challenged? Obviously, there needs to be a lot of communication between the parent and the child. This does not mean that the parent needs to sit in on every practice session—parents with several children couldn't anyway—but that parents need to be aware of what their children are feeling.

We want to be careful to look at the long-term picture. We want our children to work hard and persevere, but we don't want such a laborious struggle in their practice time that they are turned off to a long-term love of music.

Since we are now touching on such topics as hard work and perseverance, in this next section we come to the crux of the matter.

IN SEARCH OF SELF-DISCIPLINE: THE ESSENCE OF PRACTICING

To ask the question, "How does a student develop internal, self-motivating discipline?" is to ask, "How does a child develop into an adult?" It is a central element in the maturing process. Some of it can be encouraged and coaxed, but, ultimately, such maturing does take time. But it will assist the parent to at least know the basic parameters of this long-term phenomenon.

Christopher Parkening put it this way in *The Christopher Parkening Method, Vol. 2* (his advanced guitar instruction book):

For me as a Christian, self-discipline is first of all to obey the Word of God—the Bible. It is to bring my desires and my feelings and all that is in my life under the control of God supremely, so that I live an obedient life that has as its goal the glory of God. For me it includes everything from practicing the guitar with diligence to living out my spiritual life by example....

Self-discipline means nothing more than to order the priorities of your life. It is the bridge between thought and accomplishment, the glue that binds inspiration to achievement.

EXTERNAL VS. INTERNAL MOTIVATION

The great goal of teaching self-discipline is to gradually exchange the external motivation surrounding a child for internal motivation coming from *within* that child.

Step-by-step we must remove the external enforcements of the parent and teacher as the internal impetus within the child begins to activate. During this process both the teacher and the parent must, in effect, work themselves out of a job, to the point they are no longer needed. Their goal is to instill such a desire for music that a self-motivated child can take off on his own steam.

A very young child is given 100 percent external motivation: "You practice now." The child has no choice, and at his age he should have no choice. But if a senior-high student still requires that much external motivation, something is drastically wrong.

How does one gradually maneuver a child away from needing 100 percent external motivation? Every child is different, so whatever approach you take must be altogether customized. But there are some general principles to observe.

Ask yourself, *"Why* do I do the things I do?" Obviously, because we *desire* the results of our actions. Otherwise, we would do very little.

So one of the goals we are aiming for is: We want our children to *want* to play music, the results that come from practicing and practicing itself.

Rather than concentrate on the present toil, we need to help the student focus on the *results* of practicing, which are very desirable. Our train of thought might be something like this:

"If you practice well this week, you'll learn this entire piece. Then you can play before your friends, and you'll gain the respect of the whole class. You'll feel great about yourself and you'll learn to love the music, too."

This is the kind of positive message we need to be sending consistently to our children. But it is a long process, in which we give such messages regularly, that gradually takes our external motivation and turns it into our child's internal discipline.

Of course, it is difficult to cover thoroughly in a few paragraphs a process that often takes years to complete. But if we know the goal we are striving toward, we are much more likely to attain it. The object is to encourage, inspire, and enliven our children to become inwardly motivated, to need us (and our external motivation) less—to become their own teachers, coaches, and disciplinarians.

This long-term teaching should, of course, be coupled with a great deal of prayer. There are many times when, rather than constantly correcting them, we need to stop and pray for our children. In this way we allow God's power—which is far stronger than our own—to help change our childrens' lives.

As we succeed in this task, we will gain much more than good practice sessions. We will have the joy and satisfaction of watching our children mature into responsible human beings.

Making It Work for *You* —Try This:

1. Does your child like to practice? If so, go to the next chapter. But if not, examine the seven principal reasons that many kids complain about practicing. Do they fit your situation? Can you apply any of the ideas given in this chapter to help solve your child's practicing obstacles?

2. Ask your child in a practice session, "Do you know *how* to practice?" Or perhaps, "Did your teacher explain how to

practice this particular lesson?" (Discuss this fully; don't let him get off by trying to blame the teacher for everything!)

3. Consider the practicalities of your child's practicing: the location (and its freedom from distractions), the time of day, the amount of time, etc. Are these well suited for your child? If not, what can you do to make the situation better?

4. Discuss the process of acquiring self-discipline with your children.

Chapter Eight

Musical Friends, Schools, and Ensembles

◆ ◆ ◆

"How can my child make the most of his musical opportunities?"

I f you want a piece of charcoal to burn with intensity, what should you do? You could douse it with lighter fluid, light it repeatedly, blow on it—and eventually, you will have one piece of hot charcoal. By itself, it would not produce much heat, and it might go out long before its potential heating capacity is spent.

However, if you have a heap of other coals nearby, which have long since been lit and are all burning intensely, your solitary piece of charcoal would do well to join them. Then its potential heating capacity will be used to the fullest.

Your musical child is a bit like that solitary piece of charcoal. And the burning heap of coals is like the many musical friends your child can find in the various ensembles and schools in your area. Standing alone, your child may never reach his full musical potential. By joining together with other musically interested children, he will be able to experience tremendous benefits that only a group setting can provide.

This concept is true for every young musician, including

pianists. As I mentioned in chapter four, the piano-playing child has a special challenge when it comes to finding an ensemble. Many of them join choruses, which can be a marvelous experience. Some play in small groups and some play piano duets. But *all* musicians need to play with others in some capacity. "No man is an island," and that is true for musical kids, too.

FINDING *OTHER* MUSICAL KIDS

This is absolutely essential. If your little Sam does not know any other clarinet students, you may be in trouble. He will start to wonder why none of his friends take lessons. He will assume that it is because his peers disapprove of this idea. Then Sam, who could have become a talented clarinet player, may begin a campaign to quit his clarinet lessons.

But if Sam's best friend Mark is also taking clarinet lessons, you're in business. They will challenge each other, create contests and games between each other, and even spend time playing duets. The combination of musical learning and fun that occurs in such circumstances is phenomenal.

In fact, this can be a major factor in determining which instrument is best for your child. Think about it: does it really matter to you that much *which* instrument he plays, as long as he loves it? Certainly, *all* instruments are worthwhile when played well. If he is more motivated toward the clarinet than the viola, or the bass rather than the trumpet, let him choose the one that will provide him with the best chance for a positive musical experience.

If you want your Beth to begin an instrument, and her friend down the street (whom Beth adores) is taking cello lessons, then why not consider cello lessons for Beth?

On the other hand, if you already know that Beth has

another friend who has an incredible talent for piano (and has been studying it for years), you might want to encourage Beth in a different instrument. Why put her in a position where she will always be in someone else's shadow? If she chooses the flute, violin, or any other instrument, she may have a great time playing duets with her pianist friend someday.

Certainly, this principle can work for you, even if your child and his friend are studying different instruments. My son Chris is the only kid in his class who is learning the violin. But another boy, Michael, takes cello lessons, and they can still play together with the same splendid results. They carpool to their youth orchestra together and have a great time arguing over which is better: the violin or the cello. (I know. *I* drive the carpool, and you've never heard such laughable debates in your life!)

MUSICAL SIBLING RIVALRY?

If you have more than one child, you may want to expose each of them to music in his own way. As every parent knows, each child you have is unique. Therefore, give each child the personalized guidance he needs to explore and discover his own musical path.

For example, if your firstborn Sara plays the piano, you might consider sending your secondborn George to a teacher of the clarinet, violin, or trumpet. Otherwise, he may be discouraged when he can never quite play as well as Sara, who has several years of lessons ahead of him. Or worse, George may be extra talented, pass up Sara, and make her feel like giving up what was otherwise a positive experience.

Peer contests between musical friends (of approximately the same age) can be very motivating and helpful. But between siblings of different ages, playing the same instrument can be problematic because they will tend to compare one another's abilities too often.

For instance, some children are late bloomers while others show their talents at a very early age. Be careful not to let your children discourage one another with their comparisons. Your six-year-old Mary Jeane may show tremendous talent after only a few lessons, while your ten-year-old Jim may show little promise after four years of lessons. Yet, because he has been at it longer, Jim presently sounds much better on the instrument than the beginner Mary Jeane. Kids may mischievously bring this fact to everyone's attention—discouraging Mary Jeane in the process. But if Jim and Mary Jeane are playing different instruments, such juvenile comparisons aren't as likely to sting her.

Whatever you decide for your children, treat each as an individual and without partiality. And please never think of considering the notorious practice of sending one child to music lessons so that he can pass on his knowledge to another child. If you want two children to experience music, make sure each has the individual attention and musical expertise of a teacher. Don't expect a child to absorb much secondhand—forcing one child to teach another can be detrimental to the music experience of all involved!

FINDING THE RIGHT ENSEMBLES FOR YOUR CHILDREN

Once you have your children playing their respective instruments, it's important to get them playing with other children. This idea works easily enough if you live in a large metropolitan area and know hundreds of people in your community, church, or workplace. As I mentioned in chapter six, if your child takes private lessons through a music school, he can often join ensembles in that school.

But suppose you don't have any of these possibilities. You

may have some searching to do. The musical networking you will engage in, however, will enable you to meet all sorts of new friends. This is true both for the student and for the parent as you meet other parents concerned about providing musical opportunities for their children.

Of course, thousands of children are brought together in their school music programs. But some schools have very little in the way of music ensembles, and the thousands of children in smaller private schools or homeschool programs may have even fewer musical choices. Therefore, parents of those students must get involved to find the best possible opportunities for their children to play music with others.

Even if a child goes to a school with a good music program, including choruses, bands, and orchestras, there are still other possibilities you may want to consider:

Youth orchestras. Youth orchestra programs are invaluable to the young musician. If it is possible, have your child be a member of one, and give the group your total support. Through these organizations, kids are introduced to the great masters such as Bach, Beethoven, and Brahms—and they love it! The thrill of performing in a massive orchestra (with many friends) is a tremendous learning experience.

Many youth orchestra programs have several orchestras in order to accommodate children of different ages, grade levels, or musical abilities. There might be a beginning orchestra, an intermediate one, and an advanced one. Newcomers often start in one of the lower groups and work their way to the top. No matter which orchestra your Sally plays in, her musical experience will be enriched by the great musical things that begin to happen.

Bands. For wind and percussion players, a band can be as much fun as an orchestra. Orchestras need dozens of string players but only two to four of each wind instrument, and very few percussionists. Yet a marching band can put them all to work and be a wonderful time as well. Furthermore, many band programs have their own instruments, which can give your child an easy opportunity to try one.

Some kids like the fun of marching bands, where they must practice the marching as well as the music. Many of the more serious musicians prefer a concert band, where the music is more challenging and the rehearsals air-conditioned. In either case, kids are given the opportunity of musically working together with their friends.

Chamber groups. Although these groups use fewer children—anywhere from three to ten or so—they present new challenges for parents. You may have to form them by yourself.

Your community may already have a youth orchestra program or a community band. But for your child to play in a string quartet, you must find three other kids as close to your child's playing ability as possible.

A young group needs to have a teacher, or "coach," to help them in this endeavor. You could ask the school music teacher or a private teacher to direct them. (If the parents of each child split the expense of the teacher's fee, it won't be much of a financial strain on anyone.) A group of older students can play together without assistance, but they occasionally should find a coach for a chamber music session.

Let me assure you that this musical experience can be so rewarding that it's worth the extra effort. Certainly, by the time your children reach senior high school, every one of them should have had the fantastic experience of playing in a chamber music group. Try encouraging three to five kids in a youth orchestra who are close friends to get together and play. Suggest a "chamber music party" at a friend's house, or make and help to provide an opportunity for your child to discover this beautiful means of making music.

Choruses or choirs. Even if your child is an oboist, a violinist, a percussionist, or a bass player, have him seriously consider joining a vocal ensemble. Certainly, these are a must for children who naturally love to sing. But they are also a valuable experience for instrumentalists, especially for those who do not have the occasion to play in instrumental ensembles. Young pianists certainly should join a vocal group, which will greatly strengthen their musicality.

Obviously, if your church has a choir that allows children, you've got it made. Have your child join—or better yet, why don't you *both* join? This will enhance his or her musical life and can enrich your family's spiritual life as well!

If this is not an option, see if there are community choruses in your vicinity. If all else fails, perhaps you could organize a group of children to sing together regularly. Surely *someone* you know has enough musical ability to arrange this.

One final note about these ensemble possibilities. Even if your child does not attend the public school that has the best music programs in your area, it may still be possible to utilize them in your child's musical education. Many orchestra, band, and chorus directors will allow a talented student who does not attend the school to join an ensemble. It's certainly worth asking. After all, it will help the ensemble—and it's *your* taxes that are paying for the music program anyway.

SELECTING THE RIGHT SCHOOL MUSIC PROGRAMS

If your children go to the public school down the street, this topic may seem a moot point. Naturally they must be in *that* school music program.

Even if that is the case, there are still some choices you can make. To begin with, you may have the same ensemble possibilities we just discussed. Your Sally is required to take courses in such subjects such as algebra, history, and English. She will probably not have the time to sing in the chorus *and* play flute in both the school band and orchestra. Some hard choices have to be made.

Whatever options and choices confront you, there are three people with whom *every* parent should talk if they have children in school music programs:

1. Talk to the *school principal* about the music program. Tell the principal how important it is to you and your family. Express your concern that the program receive strong support from the school. Once you have your child in the program, make sure the principal knows how much you appreciate the music teacher(s) and conductor(s).

2. Talk to the *music teacher(s) and conductor(s)* about their music program. Tell them how important music is to you and your child. Ask about their expectations and requirements of the students. Ask them how you as a parent can support them. When opportunities present themselves, offer to help in various capacities. Be prepared to sell a truckload of candy during the annual fundraising event!

3. Talk to *your child* about the music program he is entering. Make sure he takes it seriously and is willing to do the work and practicing required. Explain clearly the expectations that you and the teacher(s) or conductor(s) have. Encourage your child as much as possible to achieve the best results.

These "talks" are equally important when a child enters *any* ensemble. Parents should certainly communicate with and encourage the directors of youth orchestras, bands, and choruses, whether or not they are in school programs. The people who work with your children need motivation too, and all teachers appreciate a kind, complimentary word from a supportive parent.

Of course, the primary person you are to encourage is your child, who needs your respect and reassurance to prosper. Even simple things, such as how you address him in public, can go a long way to building up your child's musical self esteem. Instead of introducing your budding violinist as "John, who takes violin lessons," speak of him as "John, who is *a violinist.*"

A little admiration and praise with a child, as with adults, will go a long way.

Making It Work for *You* —Try This:

1. Make a list of your child's musical friends. If it's a long list, bravo! Proceed to the next chapter. If not, try some of the suggestions in this chapter to help your child find a few new friends who love music.

2. Find all the musical ensembles (vocal and instrumental) in your community. If your kids are not already involved in at least one, work out a way to join up soon. If none exist in your community, get together with some interested parents and organize one!

3. Talk with your child about his or her school music program. Is it acceptable to both of you? What can you do to improve the situation?

4. Set up appointments to talk to your school's music teacher(s) and principal. Ask them for suggestions on how you can best support their music program.

Chapter Nine

Performing: "Do I Really Have to Bow?"

♦ ♦ ♦

"How can my child truly shine in musical performances?"

Imagine a football team that practices each week but never plays a game against another team. Imagine owning a fine car that you start each morning but never take out of the driveway. Or a school that teaches every day but never gives any tests or grades. (Don't read that last sentence to your children—they'd probably love it!)

In reality, none of the above situations ever happens, or ever should happen. In the same way, the process of learning music is more than a meaningful exercise. Music was made to be performed! It was meant to be shared with others. Whether the setting is Carnegie Hall or your living room, music was written to be played for the benefit of those in an audience.

This may seem obvious to you. Yet there are thousands of music students across the country who will go for many months–or even years–without performing. There are even teachers (I'm sorry to report) who don't require their students to give a recital of the pieces they have learned. I want to ask them: "What good is it to work for hours and hours to learn great music, only to discard it without performance and simply move on to another work?"

This is not to say that sitting alone and playing your instrument for the joy of it is inherently wrong. Indeed, as a classical guitarist, some of my greatest happiness is found by playing Bach in moments of solitude. (With four children, this doesn't often happen!) It is certainly a delight to spend time playing music without listeners for the ecstasy of the music itself.

However, if this is done exclusively, one cannot help but feel a bit selfish. If the music is so beautiful for you to hear, why not share it with others? Why keep all the joy to yourself?

Furthermore, there is a dimension to playing music that is only found through performing for an audience. The great violinist, Isaac Stern, once noted that a piece one has learned is "like a cake yet unbaked," until it is played before an audience. You might say that the hours of practicing adds all the ingredients together, but until it is baked no one can enjoy it.

Music was written to be performed!

THE IMPORTANCE OF PERFORMING *FREQUENTLY*

Remember that long list of benefits from a music education that I cited in chapter one? There is *no* substitute for performing frequently if a musician is to reap these tremendous rewards. Good experiences in performing, on the other hand, can tremendously benefit a child's confidence and self-esteem as well as his ability to overcome his fears.

It is possible to learn perseverance and discipline by merely working on a piece of music. But if your children seldom perform, they miss a valuable lesson in overcoming public fears that could aid them throughout life. In fact, those who refuse to perform, yet continue to learn piece after piece, often *enforce* their fear of failure.

When I interviewed the many professional performers and teachers whose ideas I often quote in this book, one topic that *every single master* felt strongly about was the importance of frequent performing. As guitarist Christopher Parkening asserted, "*All* music students should take advantage of *every* performance opportunity to refine their performing skills."

A student is never too young to start performing. (Keep in mind that "performing" does not always refer to a large concert hall or a formal audience.) A little guy can play his latest piece for his sister, mom, or friend.

Neither does the performance have to be very long and formal. Whenever a tiny accomplishment is made—a few notes in the right order, a tricky little rhythm, even a decent tone quality—the result can be immediately displayed for all to see and applaud. This becomes the best fuel for accomplishing the next little task.

Setting up such impromptu performances shows the child that his parents are proud of him and his accomplishments. Christopher Parkening's father constantly asked his son to perform for relatives and friends. Once, the young Parkening was even awakened from sleep by his father, who asked him to play for some friends who had dropped in. Perhaps this drowsy performance was not his best, but Parkening never forgot such encouragements that his parents always gave him.

In fact, the sooner a young musician starts performing, the better. It is much easier for a preschooler to give his first performance than for a new music student in junior high. The older child, without previous performing experience, is likely to be self-conscious and afraid of failure (especially in front of his peers). But when a child begins performing early enough, he doesn't yet know that he should be nervous! Confidence can gradually increase so that composure is assured long before the child grows into greater peer-awareness.

Since most of us have many obstacles to overcome in producing a satisfactory performance, the temptation might be to avoid performances altogether. But as opera singer Myra Merritt points out, "The more we perform, the more we overcome!"

ARE YOU SHY, NERVOUS, OR BOTH?

You may recall that in the first chapter I mentioned that, according to many surveys, the number-one fear for many people is public speaking. Apparently, many otherwise happy adults live in terror of the thought of standing up before a group and giving a talk.

The musical equivalent of public speaking is performing, or perhaps solo performing. Yes, it can be rather unnerving, especially for the naturally reserved child. But it does not have to be so forever; it can be overcome.

Entire books have been written about the problem of stage-fright and nervousness. To simplify the issue, James Buswell notes that there are two primary types of nervous performers:

1. Those who are nervous because they are unprepared.
2. Those who are nervous because they are self-conscious.

When he encounters students that are nervous for the first reason, Buswell tells them that he is *glad* they are nervous, since it might motivate them to be better prepared!

In fact, if you ask any great performer about the subject of nervousness, they will start talking about the importance of preparedness. Andrés Segovia acknowledged that a performer could lose up to 50 percent of his technique due to nerves. All teachers and performers point out that the best cure for *future* nervousness is *present* preparation.

It is to those students with the latter problem—too much

self-consciousness—that the books and clinical studies on nervousness have been written. Most, however, are only necessary for the rare person who, even after years of performing in front of people, is still terrified of the prospect.

If your child is extra nervous before a performance, as a parent you will want to determine the reason for it. Is it simply a lack of preparation? If so, then back to the practice room! That little extra practice might be all it takes to remedy the situation.

But if you sense that little Bobby is feeling overly self-conscious, try to help him in that area. Encourage him to focus on the music, and not on himself and what he imagines that others may think of him. Maybe a little humor will help him to lighten up, reducing the tension level. Spend some time praying with him and trying to calm and reassure him.

Another aid to lower the irrational fears that self-consciousness can produce is to have him change his point of focus by memorizing scriptures that bring him peace. Some of the best for this are:

"You will keep in perfect peace him whose mind is steadfast, because he trusts in you" (Is 26:3).

"Great peace have they who love your law, and nothing can make them stumble" (Ps 119:165).

"Peace I leave with you; my peace I give you. I do not give to you as the world gives. Do not let your heart be troubled and do not be afraid" (Jn 14:27).

"I have told you these things, so that in me you may have peace. In this world you will have trouble. But take heart! I have overcome the world" (Jn 16:33).

"And the peace of God, which transcends all understanding, will guard your hearts and minds in Christ Jesus" (Phil 4:7).

PERFORM WHENEVER POSSIBLE

The average human being can learn to adapt to almost any-thing—even performing without anxiety—if it is done fre-quently enough. In most cases the level of a child's anxiety is *inversely proportional* to how frequently he or she performs.

Do you remember when you first learned to drive a car? At first it may have been a disconcerting experience (for both you *and* your driving coach!). Yet after a few months of frequent dri-ving, it became second nature and the fear gradually vanished.

But suppose that, after you initially learned to drive, you were allowed to drive a car only one day each year. Certainly, that day each year would be accompanied by a highly acceler-ated heartbeat. You would probably be so careful (or rather, fearful) that you would not do your best.

And yet, it is not uncommon for young music students to go months without performing for others. They learn their instruments and their compositions, and they are told to wait, wait, wait for a chance to use them. No wonder they're ner-vous when they finally perform!

THREE DIFFERENT TYPES OF PERFORMANCES

There are all kinds of performance opportunities, each with different pros and cons. Playing in a huge violin section of an orchestra, for example, is a very different feeling than giving a solo recital before a large, quiet crowd. In the first situation, unless you make a glaring blunder, only your stand partner and the conductor will notice. (You may even stop playing without anyone taking notice!) But in the latter case, every little note—including every possible mistake—is instantly exposed to the ears of everyone.

Because of this "safety in numbers" factor, a child who is

naturally shy will feel more comfortable in a large ensemble (vocal or instrumental) than in a solo recital. As I pointed out in the last chapter, parents of *all* musical children, especially nervous ones, should place their children in ensembles such as an orchestra or a chorus. This way a child's confidence level can build until he or she is ready to try something a little more exposed.

Trombonist James Kraft developed a formula that clearly links "exposure" and "preparedness" to nervousness in performing: "Nervousness is *inversely* proportional to the amount of preparedness of the student, and it is *directly* proportional to the *exposure* of that student in that performance." Thus, the more a fearful student can be submerged in a large group of fellow musicians, the easier he can get over his fears of performing and begin to develop self-confidence.

A second type of performance is that of the small ensemble, otherwise known as chamber music. Whether instrumental or vocal, these groups may contain anywhere from three to about twelve performers. Players' individual contributions are more consequential than in the large groups. As you might imagine, the individual's musical part is usually more challenging in these chamber music ensembles.

A third type of performance is that of the soloist. Although this is surely the most difficult type, it is all too common for many young musicians (particularly pianists) to be familiar *only* with the solo recital. Except for a slight piano accompaniment, there is nothing to hide behind. All the responsibility and the spotlight is on you and you alone. Gulp!

The reason I have outlined the topic in this way is to point out the advantages of *all* these types of performances. While some instruments lend themselves more readily to one type of performance or another, the student's performing experience should never be limited by such factors.

For example, all string students (who normally spend so

many hours playing in orchestras) need to give solo recitals and play chamber music. Every student who truly wants to sing needs to do more than simply be in a choir or school chorus—he or she should perform solos and duets. And *every* pianist needs to perform with other musicians: chamber music, accompaniments, anything! Otherwise, the lone pianist can become musically ingrown, unable to flow with other musicians, and even the sensitivity in her solo playing begins to suffer.

I mentioned that for the naturally shy child, it might be well to work in ensembles rather than just occasional (and terrifying) solo recitals. But what about pianists?

One of the easiest ways for a bashful pianist to overcome his fears is to begin playing piano duets with a friend or family member. Music written or arranged for "one piano, two players" is known as, "piano, four hands." There are great pieces and wonderful arrangements for such an "ensemble." It's fabulous for teaching musicality as well as helping the shy student gain confidence in performing.

I witnessed two very timorous young pianists—each horrified by the thought of a solo recital—who came together for a duet with sidelong, demure smiles, as if to say, "Well, I'll do it if you will!" Before long, they were joyfully playing music together and learning the poise they needed to perform before an audience.

One more point concerning these different types of performing: You need to consider the personality type of your children to know which performance situations you should encourage. A reserved child will comfortably spend all his time hidden in large ensembles unless he is motivated to try a solo performance. Likewise, an outgoing child who loves to perform solos is never going to develop his musicality unless he is also encouraged to perform with other musicians.

So when you are working with the musical needs of your children, don't merely think of what they *want* to do. Consider what they *need*, what will help them along to greater musical fulfillment and excellence.

SEEK AND YE SHALL FIND:
CREATING PERFORMANCE OPPORTUNITIES

By now, some of you parents must be saying, "Why is he telling all this to *us*? My children take private lessons and play music in school. Isn't finding performance opportunities their teachers' responsibility?"

No. The number one reason that most students perform so infrequently is because the parent assumes, mistakenly, that setting up performance possibilities is always the music teacher's task. But the students who perform the most, and usually improve the most rapidly, are those whose parents are very involved with their performances.

Your daughter Anna's private viola teacher, Mrs. Lambert, may have thirty to fifty other private students. Believe me, Mrs. Lambert is doing quite well if she can arrange to have her students give *one* joint recital every year. She cannot be her students' only source of performance opportunities.

Yet they still *need* to perform, so it's up to the parents to get involved. Even before Leopold Mozart was arranging concerts for his son Wolfgang, parents had long been "playing manager" to their talented children. Bach even found *jobs* for his musical children! But when I use the word "manager," I'm being somewhat facetious. I'm not suggesting that you start renting out the biggest concert hall in your town. You simply need to be on the lookout for performance possibilities, however unforeseen.

Let me give you a few examples you might consider for your children:

- When relatives or guests drop in, ask if your child can play his latest piano piece for them. When he finishes, applaud à la Carnegie Hall.

- If you have more than one musical child, have a duet ready for them to perform in the above situation. Or maybe a trio, or a quartet, or... how many children do you have, anyway?

- Have a regular "family night" concert, where everyone (including Mom and Dad!) has to perform something for one another. Those who have not studied music can give a dramatic reading of a poem or story, a one-man skit, or an athletic demonstration.

- Every time a new piece is mastered, make a cassette tape of it. The collection will be a fabulous gift for grandparents, and provide a good indication of the student's progress.

- Speaking of making a tape, how about a *video* tape? Borrow or rent a video camera for any recitals, or tape some of the activities above. Grandparents love these things! (Because children grow up very quickly, years from now these tapes will be cherished family treasures.)

- Ask whoever is in charge of the music at your church if your child can play an especially well-learned solo one Sunday morning, perhaps as a prelude or postlude to the service.

- Contact local nursing homes. They would probably love to have your children come and give a little recital—either instrumental or vocal—for their residents.

- Check out every possibility for a local youth orchestra or band program. These are a must for young instrumentalists.

- Check out every possibility for a local choir or youth chorus, whether in a church (it doesn't necessarily have to be *your* church), school, or civic organization. These are a must for young singers *and* instrumentalists.

- Start a youth choir or ensemble at your church. It could really take some of the load off your overworked choir director and be a blessing to the kids as well as the congregation.

- Contact parents of other musical children you know and arrange for a joint recital. Borrow space from your church or community center, or rent it for a reasonable price. Put up simple photocopied posters all over town.

- Offer to organize a recital for your child's busy music teacher. Let the teacher pick the pieces to play while you find the location, print the programs, and do the other legwork. (Don't forget refreshments! If you sell them, they can offset any costs of the recital.)

These are only a few of the many possibilities that can encourage your child's performing. I hope that they cause you to think about many other ideas that apply to your specific situation. Nearly anything is possible!

A WORD OF COUNSEL FOR THE FAMILY IMPRESARIO

Since you may now be energized to become your family's impresario (concert manager), let me give you a little advice. Your purpose is to encourage your child through successful performing. You should never force the student to perform when he is not well prepared. A poorly prepared student is a disaster waiting to happen, and such negative experiences will be remembered for a long time. In planning events, make sure to give young performers adequate time to prepare and feel confident.

Another potential discouragement to avert is what I call the "empty seat syndrome." It's not very encouraging to play to an audience of predominately empty seats (not to mention the frustration of working hard on a recital, putting up notices everywhere—only to have no one show up).

How can you avoid this? There are ultimately two ways to get an audience sitting in those seats: Either ask an audience to come to your concert, *or plan the concert in a place where there is already an audience.*

Sadly, most people try only the first method, which is rather precarious unless you know what you are doing. Too often, concerts are planned without regard for "audience draw": The program is planned according to what the performers know how to play (rather than what the audience wants to hear), inadequate publicity is done—and everyone naively assumes that the seats will be filled to overflowing. When this happens the results are often disappointing.

Why not try the second method instead? *Think*: where would there be a group of people who would like to be entertained with a little music? Perhaps at a church service, in a picnic lunch area or modest restaurant, or a nursing home or hospital? You would be amazed into how many situations your mini-recitals would fit.

When one of my sons was only six years old, he performed for thousands of people and they loved it! At Carnegie Hall? No, at Christmastime in a shopping mall. His resourceful piano teacher contacted the mall and arranged to have a beautiful grand piano and an excellent sound system on hand. Each of her students got to play a Christmas carol for the passersby. After my cute little Peter performed his rendition of "Jingle Bells," the crowd burst into applause—led by two very proud parents! Talk about encouragement!

So consider looking for a ready-made audience. But for those times when you do set up a formal concert, never assume that people will just show up. Work hard on publicity; it seldom takes much money, but it does involve lots of work. Put up notices *everywhere*, from local supermarkets to offices and churches. Call and invite everyone you can think of. Perhaps even send notices to your local newspaper (for their free "calendar" section) and radio stations (public service announcements are also free). Try everything to get a good crowd. When you see those empty seats filled, then the work will be well worth it.

One final admonition: Although I want to encourage you to get your children performing, remember that *they are still children.*

There will be times when your child has too much crowding in on him, and he doesn't need the extra stress of a recital. I have seen some children who are pushed so much they practically have ulcers. Watch your children. Be on the lookout for such signs as sleeplessness, lack of appetite, hyperactivity, or exhaustion. Be sensitive to the needs of your children—don't put them under undue stress. There is a balance to everything, and we need to find it for each of our children.

Incidently, in answer to the question posed in the title of this chapter: "Yes, you *do* have to take a bow after performing!"

Making It Work for *You* —Try This:

1. Count up the number of performances your children have been involved with in the last year. Do you think this is enough? Do they? How could you provide additional opportunities?

2. Talk to your children about performing. Are they especially nervous? Why? Do you think they would still be if they performed much more often?

3. Find out what ensemble possibilities are available for your children. Can you think of other children who could play and perform duets, trios, or quartets together with them?

4. Write down a number of ways your children could perform more often, right in your own home.

5. Determine to create your own recital, using your children and others you know. Set a date, find a location, plan the program, advertise, and go for it!

Interlude Two:

For Parents of Singers

◆ ◆ ◆

I f you are the parent of a budding singer, I congratulate you! But I hope you didn't simply turn to this section without reading any previous chapters of this book. Much of the material, such as the chapters on practicing and performing, relates to every young musician—instrumentalists and vocalists alike. So when you read this section, I will be taking for granted that you have familiarized yourself with the previous material.

As you have noticed throughout this book, several musical experts have helped me by giving their views and firsthand experience on many topics. Although I have conducted many vocal compositions—from the great oratorios to twentieth-century opera—I am not a singer myself. Therefore, my research includes many discussions of vocal training with many singer friends, including some of the finest singers and teachers in the country.

It may or may not surprise you to discover that almost every singer has different opinions about singing, and especially about the teaching of singing. Why is this?

Singing is a very *personal* art. When you are a singer, *you* carry your instrument *inside* you, so you are truly intimate with the producer of the music. More than any other, the singer's art is very individualized and somewhat difficult to write about conclusively.

Perhaps this personal nature of singing explains the lack of agreement among the experts as well as the paucity of standardized teaching technique.

However, there are still a number of important matters on which the experts do agree, and these are the essence of this section. Even when the great singers and teachers disagree, their conflicting conclusions are worth noting. Some of this information will apply to your family and some may not, but it's all a fascinating way of thinking about the oldest way of music- making: the human voice.

WHEN SHOULD MY CHILD START VOICE LESSONS?

Let's start with a controversial point, guaranteed to promote a raving argument among singers and vocal teachers. I've gotten opinions that range from beginning at a very young age to a very old one. I've even heard from one top singer that *all* vocal lessons are a waste of time, since, in his opinion, no one can teach singing anyway!

But almost *no* one recommends sending young children, especially boys, to voice lessons. Their "instrument"—that is, their body—is physically not ready until the teen years. A five-year-old can pick up a flute since the flute itself has already finished growing! But the human instrument known as the voice goes through many growth changes for the first twelve years or so of a person's life.

Different teachers will start students at different ages. Some start girls at twelve and boys at fifteen. Others hold a minimum age of sixteen for girls and nineteen for boys. Many voice teachers will not even consider a pre-college student. To those from an instrumental background, where child prodigies are performing professionally in their teens, this delay in vocal training seems quite unusual.

Many of the world's greatest singers (especially men) did not even start their careers until well after college. The great Metropolitan Opera basso Jerome Hines says that he was a chemistry major in college, and had never even considered singing until he was sixteen. He stumbled onto a great teacher, the renowned Gennaro Curri, and within a few years, was singing at the Met. Who knows? It might happen to *your* child, too.

The only serious exceptions to this age principle are those "child stars" who must sing in movies, shows, and commercials. A singer friend of mine in New York, Steven Schnurman, teaches a few of these young stars and can testify to their particular vocal problems. Most of their lesson time is spent training them to sing in tune. Many of these talented kids will completely ruin their voices by bellowing out notes without the proper muscular support. It's a high price to pay for getting into a movie.

Nevertheless, all vocal teachers strongly encourage youngsters of every age to sing, and sing a lot! Although it is true that many of the world's great singers did not enter serious vocal study at an early age, *all* of them sang as children. The foremost exhortation is that kids should sing *naturally*, without strain, undue volume, and without imitating anyone else—*especially* rock and roll screamers. Remember, those guys get paid to ruin their voices, but you should not let the same fate befall your child.

PIANO LESSONS: A SINGER'S SECRET WEAPON

Another point of agreement among vocal experts is the importance of learning to play an instrument. Most of the fine singers I know have played the violin, the flute, or (most frequently) the piano.

I said earlier that many vocal teachers will not accept young students. But they don't simply send them away. They send them to a piano teacher. Their typical admonition is, "Take five years of piano lessons, and then give me a call about vocal training."

Since the mechanics of the voice are rather difficult to see, relating to a "visual" instrument is very helpful to a singer. The nonvisual process of singing often involves finding notes "right out of the air," so many young singers are somewhat jealous of the oboist or clarinetist who, (according to the singer) "simply pushes the right button and the right note comes out."

Playing an orchestral instrument can be an illuminating experience for a young singer. The only ensembles many vocalists ever know are the church choir or school chorus, so performing in an orchestra or band will expand their musical horizons. It also teaches the importance of intonation, blending, balance, good rhythm, and following the conductor.

But even if other instruments are not readily available, *all* singers *must* learn to play piano, at least in some capacity. Everything vocal seems related to the piano. Piano proficiency will help a singer to learn melodies, to accompany himself and others, and to expand his knowledge of the huge repertoire of music for voice and keyboards.

So if your little Wayne is a potential Caruso but is too young to start serious vocal training, do him a favor: start Wayne on piano lessons.

THE IMPORTANCE OF MUSIC THEORY FOR SINGERS

This is a critical subject for *every* singer, and yet many singers seem almost afraid of it. Knowing the basics of music theory is a *must* for a good singer, and it will set him apart from all the rest. In church choirs and even in music schools, it's almost tragic how many young singers sound wonderful—yet can hardly read the music they sing!

This problem can seriously hinder many excellent young singers. Without music theory, it can take weeks to learn a short piece that should have been sight-reading material. Without music theory, singers often don't know if they are out of tune, or even *why* they are out of tune. Without music theory, singers are burdened to learn everything "by ear," which can terribly limit their repertoire.

When a student has a solid background in music theory, he or she will be able to decode the "whys" and "hows" of music: why a melody moves in various directions, how to find opening pitches, and why a composer has chosen certain harmonies in a piece of music. Music theory is essential in the process of music *interpretation*, since it endeavors to answer such key questions as, "*Why* did the composer write this rhythm, or this harmony, or this melodic phrase?"

Let me give you an analogy. My wife is a gourmet cook, so she ad-libs fantastic recipes, throwing in "a dash of this and a pinch of that." When I bungle into the kitchen, I have to carefully follow each line of a recipe, trying to keep my teaspoons and tablespoons straight, terrified lest I ruin the whole thing with one false move. I don't understand the "whys" behind the recipes, much to my wife's amusement. I am like the singer who doesn't know music theory, and doesn't understand the "whys" behind the music.

The basics of music theory are not difficult to learn. I have taught very young children to read music quickly, and given them more music theory than some college courses cover. Perhaps the best instrument on which to learn theory is the piano, and every respectable piano teacher adds this information to the study of that instrument.

This is also a subject that can be studied long before formal voice lessons begin. That way the young singer is more thoroughly prepared to participate in serious vocal study and will progress rapidly. So when the voice teacher refuses to take a young student and sends him to the piano, he should learn music theory as well as piano technique.

THE VOCAL REPERTOIRE

This is another subject that is very important for singers and yet is all too often neglected. Long before the years of formal voice study, a young singer can and should become familiar with the fundamental repertoire he or she would like to sing someday. An aspiring vocalist can begin to accomplish this by simply going to the library each month and returning home with an armload of CDs for that month's listening.

An obvious question a young singer should ask himself is, "What kind of music do I want to sing?" The answers can range from popular songs to Wagnerian opera, but finding the honest answer to this question is the first step for any aspiring vocalist. A vague response like, "Oh, I just want to sing everything!" is bound to create a singer who will sing nothing, at least successfully.

Once the answer to this key question is determined, two other important questions are, "What music in this chosen genre do I already know?", and "What additional music in this genre should I begin to learn?" This kind of creative thinking goes into the making of great musicians.

Certainly, these questions and many others will be addressed fully when your child works with a vocal teacher. The teacher will then guide the student through the best repertoire for the child's voice and aspirations. This is where the expertise of an excellent teacher is needed in order to point the excited young student in the right direction.

To illustrate this concept, let me give you an example.

Suppose your daughter Betty heard Handel's *Messiah* and loved it. She now dreams about singing its soprano solos and other similar pieces. Then she should buy the music and a good recording. She can learn each soprano movement, at least what they sound like, whether she is yet capable of singing them or not. Next, she should listen to similar masterpieces and become familiar with their soprano arias, such as Bach's *Magnificat,* Haydn's *Creation,* the *Requiem* of Mozart, Brahms, Faure, Verdi, and so on.

Learning the repertoire is necessary for every vocal genre, from Broadway to opera. When I see a young singer motivated to learn as much music as possible, I know that a serious musician is in the making. In fact, this kind of self-motivated learning is the best way to determine if a proclaimed desire to sing is just a whim or a significant aspiration.

Soprano Myra Merritt said she starts preparing an opera role six months before the first performance, working every day. She studies the score scrupulously, learning everything she can about the music and the text, until the music becomes a part of her. In this way, the music gradually becomes internalized.

Rather than take a haphazard approach to the huge opera repertoire, she concentrates on those roles that best fit her voice. Myra exhorts young singers to "Know the repertoire that is *for you!*" Once these works are selected, let nothing hinder you until they are all eventually mastered. Again, the singer's teacher should help find the best repertoire, but the *intense desire* to find such works must originate within the student.

One of the classic distinctions between first-rate and second-rate singers is their preparedness. Second-rate singers never learn a piece of music until they are told, by a teacher, a conductor, or a manager. First-rate singers are constantly learning pieces *before* they are ever asked to sing them. When they are finally asked, they are already prepared. Such foresight and preparation go a long way toward the making of a great singer.

Although Jerome Hines started his musical study at sixteen, by his twentieth birthday he had been thrust into learning his roles in twenty different operas. Today, he runs a prominent opera program for young singers, and his standards for them are just as high.

Sadly, many opera singers have graduated from four years of full-time music school, and yet they know only one or two operas. They have learned art songs randomly and worked on technique, but they haven't taken the time to master the principal repertoire in which they claim to want to spend their life. This lack of preparation will seriously hinder any career they might have had in singing.

This was once dramatically demonstrated to me on a professional scale. I was rehearsing one afternoon with Jerome Hines in Newark, New Jersey, when he received a frantic telephone call from the Metropolitan Opera Company. The tenor who was singing Verdi's *Don Carlo* had become suddenly ill, and they did not have a substitute available. Did he know anyone who had the role well prepared? We contacted a number of excellent tenors, only to find that none knew the part. It could have (and should have) been the career boost of a lifetime for some young singer—a starring role at the Met! But none of the singers we called had ever gotten around to learning the part. They were waiting to be asked first.

Your child might not ever sing at the Met, but preparedness in learning the vocal repertoire can begin today.

HOW CAN I FIND A GOOD VOICE TEACHER?

If you ask this question to many voice teachers, they may tell you, "There are no other good voice teachers. Here's *my* number." Try it sometime.

This is not exactly conceit. Just as singing is a very personal art, the teaching of singing is extremely personalized. Therefore, it may be difficult for you to find an excellent vocal teacher. It is certainly difficult to advise you in this matter.

Chapter 6 was primarily concerned with instrumental music lessons, but the twelve points in that chapter about how you can find a good instrumental teacher apply to this subject as well. Furthermore, there are a few additional challenges to finding a good voice teacher.

A local singer may have a beautiful voice, yet may know absolutely nothing about the teaching of vocal technique. This is less likely to happen in the instrumental world: If someone can play a bassoon well, then he must at least know how to physically play the instrument. He knows that to produce a low C, he must press certain keys, cover certain holes, and blow in a specific way. And once this is learned, the instrumentalist can show someone else how to do it. That person might not have a special gift for teaching, but he could at least convey technical information about the instrument.

On the other hand, there are those who have naturally beautiful voices and are known as excellent singers, yet they have little idea of what is going on within them. Nor would they be able to instruct someone *else* in the art of singing. At best, such a vocalist could demonstrate his voice to you and ask (but not help) you to imitate it. This is not true vocal instruction, and is not worth paying for.

I'm afraid there are also "singing teachers" whose idea of instruction is simply to listen to you sing each week and critique your performance. Although this practice can be quite helpful, this is not vocal instruction. *Any* trained musician (whether singer or tuba player) could do the same and give helpful criticism like, "You did this very well, but this was not done as well." Realize, though, that this practice is still not the same as vocal instruction.

Vocal students need to know more than, "This was great, this was bad." They need to know *HOW* to make the bad parts sound great! They need specific, technical help to change faulty vocal practices into correct ones. They need someone who's able to hear a weak passage, quickly analyze what the student is doing wrong, diagnose how to best correct the problem, clearly explain the needed correction, and help the student change as needed. They need reliable explanations for those faults that are hindering their technique. They need the ability to consistently remove these faults and to use their vocal instrument to the best of their natural ability.

All this is to say: Young singers need to find a voice teacher *who can teach vocal technique.* For example, they need to be taught breath control, specific muscular support, control of the different "voices" (chest voice, head voice, etc.), diction and facility in various languages, and a myriad of other vocal information. Be wary of teachers who speak of "intuitive singing," or explain technique by saying, "You can just *feel* it." Such vague statements often mask a lack of technical information.

Parents should always be cognizant of their children's response to their voice lessons. There are many superb voice teachers, but there are inferior ones as well. We want to make sure you get the right one for your budding singer.

Chapter Ten

"I Want to Quit!" and Other Challenges

◆ ◆ ◆

"How do we continue through the tough times?"

In the introduction to this book, I mentioned that I often hear adults who say, "If only I hadn't quit my music lessons," or even, "How I wish my parents hadn't let me quit my lessons." Perhaps you've said this yourself. For thousands of people around the world, the abandonment of music study later becomes one of life's greatest regrets.

If you are one of these adults who now wish that your parents had made you stick with it, consider it from their point of view. You may have made them miserable for months with protests and whining about lessons or practicing. They may not have had adequate counsel to help them. They may also have been short of money. Finally they reached their limit, these factors engulfed them, and your lessons ceased. One can hardly blame them.

Why do kids want to quit? Should parents let them? How long should parents make them persevere? Should kids never quit? Or is there a time when they should naturally stop taking lessons?

These are complex questions, and you can quickly become

perplexed and bewildered if you ask them of a number of people. To find answers that will benefit your family's specific situation, let's try to simplify the issue.

First of all, I want to list a few basic assumptions:

1. Education is indispensable for our children's well-being.
2. Studying music is a key component of their overall education.
3. Studying music, to be effectively learned, involves some hard work.
4. Children will, at least sometimes, refuse such hard work unless they are compelled by their parent(s).
5. Therefore, parents must insist on this hard work (overruling the child's choice) if music is to be effectually learned.

Most parents feel a responsibility to guide their children through difficult choices in their young lives; unfortunately, this guidance often involves overruling our child's wishes. There are many scriptures that point out that a parent is to "see that his children obey him with proper respect" (1 Tim. 3:4). This entire book, and certainly this chapter, is written with the basic assumption that the parent is the child's authority, and makes the decisions based on what is in the child's best interest.

This does not mean that parents should be insensitive to their children's feelings, especially as they mature. Of course we need to hear them out, discuss situations with them, and gradually grant them more and more responsibility. But when it comes to quitting music lessons, the parents *must not* abdicate their duty to their children.

I have known and worked with hundreds of young musicians for many years, at every possible level of personal maturity. In all those years, I have never met *one* who had the maturity to understand all the ramifications of continuing or quitting music lessons before he reached senior high. There are, of course, many young students who *thought* they could make this decision!

Many of these students had parents who were busy, hassled with other decisions, and tired. So when their kid announced that he wanted to quit—well, it just wasn't worth the fight.

This is exactly why so many adults out there are now saying, "If only I hadn't quit my music lessons," and, "How I wish my parents hadn't let me quit my lessons."

This is how it happens, and most of the time it shouldn't happen. All the wonderful investment of years of lessons and practicing go down the drain. Let's consider a better alternative.

PREVENTIVE MEDICINE FOR YOUNG MUSICIANS

As always, the best medicine is preventive medicine. If we as parents do the right things in our children's musical education, we may never hear the unpleasant words, "I want to quit!" Indeed, this entire book was written to help you do the right things and therefore avoid this unnecessary misadventure.

Review some of the chapters of this book. If your child wants to quit music, ask yourself such questions as, "Have I created the right home environment to nurture my child's love of music?" "Did I start his musical education off positively?" "Have I found the right teacher(s)?" "Is he in the right ensemble, school, and musical environment?" "Does he have a good practice location and time?" "Have there been opportunities to perform?" "Has he been consistently receiving the encouragement he needs?"

Perhaps a little self-reflection might reveal a minor adjustment on your part that will help your child in music. That is why I mentioned earlier the importance of really knowing your child. By detecting something early in the game, you may save your child from giving up a musical experience that will continue to enrich his life for years to come.

Although some parents may not believe it—particularly those who have had the misfortune to go through the misery of fighting their children over this issue—it is not uncommon for children to *never* want to quit. I recently asked the violinist James Buswell (who began at age five) if there was ever a time when he wanted to quit. He pondered the question, then answered, "No. Why should I have?" He was receiving so much encouragement from his parents, teachers, and friends that it would have seemed crazy to quit.

The same positive experience can happen for your child!

NO PARENTAL GUILT ALLOWED

If your children never learn to love their music lessons or practice sessions, and you experience battles over this subject, let me first relieve you of any guilt you may be feeling. You can do *everything* right with your children, applying every idea in this book and others, and still have your kids come back and yell, "I want to quit!"

This is *not* necessarily because you did something wrong. Children have their own free will, and even the best, most compliant kid can sometimes openly defy you. When King Solomon pointed out that "folly is bound up in the heart of a child," he knew what he was talking about. The resulting confrontations happen to nearly all of us.

Indeed, it certainly has happened in my family. I hope that I haven't given you an idyllic picture of the musical Kavanaugh household. My four boys have iron wills, and if they don't like something (like practicing, maybe) they let me know—loud and clear! At least once if I hadn't intervened, my son Chris would have probably broken his violin to splinters. I understand where you're at—I've been there, too.

JUNIOR HIGHERS ARE THE FOREMOST QUITTERS

Do you remember the Shakespeare play, *Julius Caesar?* The soothsayer eerily prophesies to the emperor, "Beware the Ides of March!" (Later, this prophecy comes true when Caesar is murdered on the Ides of March, that is, March 15.) Well, to parents with musical children of a young age, I sometimes feel like prophesying, "Beware the junior high years!"

Music teachers may not be child psychologists, but they all know something about junior-highers: They quit a lot. The years from about the sixth to the ninth grades seem to be a kind of gauntlet that musicians must run through in order to survive for the duration. Many of them don't make it, and this is lamentable. This difficult period of time often becomes the graveyard for many a young musician's budding progress. Even after years of happy, motivated playing, thousands of talented kids want to give it up in junior high. You would think that someone was slipping something into the water....

Child psychologists tell us that kids of this age are going through many changes. They become much more peer-related, all kinds of uproarious physical changes are exploding within them, and social encounters with the opposite sex suddenly have new dimensions. Everything they have known is affected by these changes of colossal magnitude that are touching their lives. And music lessons are often one of the unfortunate casualties.

Of course, a child of any age may want to quit for a variety of reasons. Whether your child happens to be a junior higher or not, if he yells, "I want to quit!" you've got the same problem.

WHY DOES THIS HAPPEN?

There are hundreds of bad arguments your child may give when you ask the unavoidable query, "Why do you want to quit?" But there are a few good arguments that you need to hear carefully. The key is having the wisdom to separate the bad ones from the good. And, especially in dealing with junior highers, you would do well to listen to the apostle James' injunction, "If any of you lacks wisdom, he should ask God, who gives generously to all without finding fault, and it will be given to him" (Jas 1:5).

The bad arguments for quitting lessons can range from the sublime to the ridiculous, but they are fairly easy to detect:

"I hate the trombone! Tommy said that it looks like a giant paper clip!"

"None of the girls plays it! It sounds like a freight train!"

I'm not going to spend any more time listing such reasons, because you've probably already heard them all.

However, there are some statements from your children that should get our attention and prompt action. This is *not* to say that when we hear these reasons we should suddenly acquiesce in our child's demand to quit. Far from it. But some things a child says may certainly alert you to a legitimate need or problem that must be addressed.

For example, if a child says that he hates his teacher, you should sit down with him and ask why he feels that way. There may be a personality conflict here that you weren't aware of, and sometimes action needs to be taken on your part. If you hear constant complaints about the school program, maybe you should look into what may be a real problem, warranting adult intervention. There are many possible situations in which the cry, "I want to quit!" is really your child imploring you to get involved and resolve something that truly needs to be resolved.

WHEN TO QUIT AND WHEN *NOT* TO QUIT

Let me begin by stating that there are times when your child *should* quit his music lessons, and there are times when he should not. You might say that there are *valid, positive* reasons to quit, and there are *invalid, negative* reasons to quit—or rather, *not* to quit.

It is my purpose to make the difference between these two types of reasons very clear to you. Ultimately, it is your job as a parent to discern which type of reasons are coming out of your child's mouth and act accordingly.

Therefore, I must deal with the negative reasons first, and then move on to the *valid* reasons for quitting lessons. If such negative situations are not in your family, count your blessings, then skip ahead to the section, "When Is the Appropriate Time to Quit?"

Many parents encounter (and give in to) reasons from their children that are not valid reasons for quitting music. Hundreds of parents find themselves in arguments with their children on this issue and desperately need guidance. Take heart and read on.

Most of the "quitting" situations that confront parents stem from the simple fact that all humans, particularly immature ones, tend to complain about conditions that don't bring immediate gratification. They want to quit because they're tired of all the work, or they're discouraged because of slow results, or they're being hassled by their friends.

These are what I consider "negative" reasons.

If a fatigued parent hears this whining long enough and doesn't recognize it for what it is—typical, expectable, unexceptionable human griping—he will probably break sooner or later.

When the child has defeated the parent in this manner, there is no victory for the child, or anyone else. When a child quits music in this negative way, everyone loses. Even the child, who may temporarily believe he has won a conquest, will in a decade or two be regretting and bemoaning, "If only I hadn't quit my music lessons!"

WHAT TO DO WHEN IT HAPPENS

If you as a parent find yourself in the above predicament, I have great news for you. There is a proven way of dealing with these negative situations that works wonderfully every time. It is so innovative and ingenious that my greatest marvel is that it's not universally known and used. It certainly should be.

Here is the remarkable solution. When a child comes to you and proclaims that he wants to quit, you quietly reply, "No."

Two letters, in that specific order.

When they bring to you their complaints, gripes, grievances, and protests—when they rationally explain (Note: this doesn't occur very often) their difficulties and obstacles—when they scream, whine, cry, and hold their breath until they turn blue, you quietly reply, "No."

Even when they appeal, beg, implore, beseech, adjure, petition, entreat, and plead—and do it ninety times each day, you quietly reply (ninety times each day), "No."

Let me explain.

Even if my wife and I had already decided that (for whatever reason *we* had found) my child's music lessons should soon be concluded, if that child should try to force a termination, I would not yield to his protests. This is an adult decision, and I do not want my child to leave something for a *negative* reason.

Do we want to encourage our children to be quitters? Or, do we want to teach them perseverance, steadfastness, endurance, and a strong work ethic? Surely we do not want to teach them that if things get tough, you can always quit. Such an attitude will create problems that could affect them the rest of their lives.

Yet, if we want to teach perseverance we have to model it ourselves. Are we going to let a small child wear us down? No. Determine right now that this will never happen; you'll be doing your children one of the greatest services you could ever render them as a parent.

But it is hard. Believe me, I know.

Yet I know that this principle is right and that it works. I know this from the experience of hundreds of musicians, parents, teachers, and even my own experience.

At the age of eleven, my son Chris went on a six-month tirade against the violin and his lessons. My firstborn has a incredibly strong will, and it was pure agony for us to be in the house during this trying period of friction and protest. I'll never forget one night, when he shouted in dead seriousness, "There are four things I absolutely hate: the devil, demons, hell, and the violin!" (Don't you love adolescent theology?)

My wife and I steadfastly determined not to let him get away with this, and so we became the rock on which the sea breaks, but does not move. At one point in a frenzied confrontation, I peacefully said to Chris, "Son, you've known me all your life. Do you really think that if you just somehow complain enough, I'll finally buckle under?" Chris, seeing the complete futility of his tirade, then calmed down. I made it clear that neither of us would cower to his childish wish and relinquish our parental responsibility.

Eventually, the storm cleared. Seeing that his parents were immovable, he resigned himself to the violin and soon started enjoying it slightly—though he wouldn't admit it for a while! Today he loves it, has a blast playing in a youth orchestra, and even likes to perform for his friends.

There are *so* many similar stories from *so* many people that there is indisputably a universal ten-step principle behind them all:

1. The child begins the instrument....
2. The child enjoys the initial experience....
3. The child's work increases....
4. The child does not enjoy the experience....
5. The child wants to quit....
6. The child is made to continue, despite his protests.....
7. The child becomes convinced that his parents will not give in....
8. The child resigns himself to his fate...
9. The child begins to enjoy the instrument again, as it is mastered....
10. The child is (finally!) grateful to his parents for helping him through the ordeal....

This should be, and *can* be, the natural progression for your child's musical experience. Now our Chris loves his music, and your child can too—if he or she doesn't quit.

A famous football coach was once asked the question, "What is your definition of a great coach?" After thoughtful deliberation, he answered, "A great coach is someone who makes his players do what they don't want to do, so that they can become what they *want* to become." Ponder the wisdom of this profound statement.

This is also the responsibility of the parent of musical children. Until they have worked long enough (years, not weeks) to genuinely know their abilities, and until they have the maturity to fully comprehend the consequences of major decisions, children are not qualified to make the choice of concluding their music lessons.

Indeed, how many adults would persevere through the hard work we constantly have (often with little personal satisfaction) if we were not *made to*, by the threat of the lost income. In many ways, all of us need an authority figure to keep us from giving up when the going gets rough. *We* serve as that guiding authority for our children.

If we want our children to internally assimilate such character qualities as perseverance and fortitude, then for a while we must externally enforce the endurance needed.

We must *always* hear our children out and sensitively show compassion to their discouragement, as well as help them in any other way possible. Never let your determination to stand firm turn you into a cold, unapproachable totalitarian. Our children need love, warmth, open compassion, and a listening ear. But they also need strong, mature parents, who will give them the essential leadership they need for decisions that they are not yet qualified to make for themselves.

INSTRUMENT "HOPPING"

This principle also applies to "instrument hopping," an epidemic that spreads all too easily among schoolchildren. After a few months of the oboe, Jeff wants to play the trumpet. After a few months of the viola, Amy wants to try the flute.

Do your child a favor: do *not* succumb to this tactic, either. Parents who let their kids move quickly from one instrument to the next—perhaps naively thinking that this is giving them a broader musical education—are in reality teaching their children to play all these instruments *badly*.

Often, at the first discouragement (and it *will* come), the child wants to move to another instrument. Such hopping around results in a child who, at any given time, is considerably behind the other students who have spent years concentrating on one instrument. The consequential discouragement from being the last in the section will often lead to eventual failure at music.

Nevertheless, there are times when a move to a different

instrument is in order. (It is usually *not* when the child happens to complain and ask for such a move.) Sometimes a teacher can see that the child may have a physical problem that hinders him on the instrument he is attempting to learn. Certainly, you and the teacher should know the child, his individual personality, strengths and weaknesses. You should confer together about any possibilities that might improve your child's musical experience.

For example, I know of kids who, when they started on the trombone, got nowhere, but when they moved to the guitar, had natural talent and progressed rapidly. Or vice versa. Some children seem almost born to play a specific instrument. After *a reasonable amount of time* (at least one year; consult the teacher) on the first instrument to make certain that this is not just a whim—we should endeavor to guide them to the better choice.

You'll notice that in the above example, the parent and the teacher are doing the guiding. The child is not left without direction, drifting wherever his youthful impulses and desires may take him at the moment. The key to making these changes is that they never occur as a result of vacillation or lack of steadfastness—they should take place only when the parent and teacher have determined that such a change is for the long-range benefit of the child.

WHEN *IS* THE APPROPRIATE TIME TO QUIT?

So, is there *ever* an appropriate time to conclude music lessons? Of course. It would be a strange world if everyone took private lessons every week until dying of old age. (Wow! Just think of what music teachers could earn!)

Of the thousands of adults with the regret "If only I hadn't quit my music lessons!", the majority of them quit before or during the junior-high years. Seldom do I meet an adult with that regretful line who plowed through those painful junior high years, kept taking lessons until eighteen, finally stopped, and now regrets it.

Do you know why? Because *those* clever people stayed with it long enough to really discover joy in their music. Many of them still play music as wonderfully fulfilled amateurs. They come home from their offices and sit down at the piano to unwind. They go to the best concerts in town. They are ecstatic music-lovers, who are grateful to have had such a fruitful introduction into a lifetime of the joy of music.

Now, did these people quit their music lessons? Yes, they're not taking lessons anymore, and they haven't since the end of high school.

Do I commend them for quitting? Certainly. They did the right thing.

"What?! I thought you said... !"

Let me explain.

Remember that I said there are *positive* reasons to quit, and there are *negative* reasons to quit—or rather, *not* to quit.

All of the former examples we've been discussing—the junior highers, the screamers, the instrument hoppers—were trying to quit because of negative reasons. They wanted to escape an uncomfortable position. They found themselves confronted with work they didn't want to do. They wanted to *quit*, to run away from a tough situation.

But there are also *positive* reasons when, instead of running *away* from a tough situation, you are deliberately running *toward* a more beneficial one. There are positive reasons for some children to leave music earlier than senior high school. Perhaps your daughter Linda is blossoming into a brilliant scholar or an endowed athlete, or discovers extraordinary talents in other areas. She now needs extra time to focus on those areas in which she is especially gifted.

Obviously, if Linda has been taking music for some time and

has not shown a particular talent in it, then terminating music lessons to give her more time is a viable solution. In this way, she is not quitting music for the negative reason of running away from work. She sees clearly the positive reason of leaving music in order to pursue things more appropriate for her circumstances and life goals. But, if her music experience has been an otherwise positive one, she will continue to love music for the rest of her life.

Wonderful! This is as it should be, and is a far cry from the kid who screams, "I want to quit! I hate music!"

This is the decision of a mature youth who says, in effect, "Music has been great for me. I've had a lot of fun playing music, and I'll always love it. Even as I go on to pursue my life goals, I'll always carry fantastic memories of my musical experiences."

This is one example of a positive reason for "quitting" music. Even in these positive cases, there are a few points to consider:

1. Music lessons should only cease after significant discussions with the child, thoughtful consideration on your part, and fervent prayer. It should not be a snap decision. Such a quick judgment may turn out badly. Or, even if it was the correct choice, it will give the child the impression that you take his aspirations flippantly.

2. The child should not leave music suddenly. He should continue until a customary stopping place, such as the end of the school year or semester. Until that time he will need extra encouragement to make sure he doesn't "shut down early" and give too little effort knowing the end is coming soon.

3. Always consult the music teacher. If he disagrees, take his opinion seriously, and reconsider. But, of course, you are the parent and this is your decision. Even if you have to overrule the teacher's wishes for your child, give him the courtesy of at least a month's notice before stopping lessons.

THE CHILD WITH LITTLE MUSICAL TALENT

This "positive" principle for concluding lessons can also be applied to the following distressing, but rather common situation:

In a given year's private teaching, my wife will often get a student who has very little inborn musical talent. Let's call him Larry. He's a wonderful boy with fine, supportive parents, but his lack of natural talent slows his progress to a snail's pace. My wife will work with him, trying valiantly to bring out the little talent he has, and encourage his love of music. But after a while, she feels as if she is robbing Larry's parents by taking their money for such nonproductive lessons.

What do you do? Sooner or later, she has to sit down with the parents and be honest with them. If they are supportive parents, they want what is best for Larry. They want to find his strengths and weaknesses. They may be a little disappointed to discover that Larry won't be the next Pablo Casals, but it is better to know now than to waste any more of their money and his time.

Next, the parents need to plan a strategy, to spare Larry from feeling badly about himself as well as to insure that he will not be left with a negative feeling toward music. One course might be to try another instrument, as we have already discussed. But sometimes a student is found to have little musical aptitude of *any* kind. Although it has been scientifically proven that no one is completely tone deaf, some kids are painfully close!

If your child happens to be one of these, don't just abruptly pull him out of music lessons. Ask yourself: What are his *strengths*? Maybe he should take art lessons, or join the swimming team, or take tennis lessons. Once you think of something that seems plausible, casually mention the subject to the child and note the response. Once you find an area that he seems excited about, arrange to replace the music lessons with this new area at the beginning of the next school year or semester. He will soon be engrossed in the new field, without any negative feelings about his musical experience. He may still grow up to be an avid music-lover.

IN THE MEANTIME

We've covered many of the negative and positive reasons for quitting music. For the positive cases, exit when needed, as illustrated above. In the case where your children are only providing you with negative reasons, you'll just have to hold on and pray for the storm to clear.

Alas, in the meantime, there is still a question to answer. After your tenacious little Kevin has shouted, "I want to quit!" for the eight-hundredth time, and after you have quietly said, "No" for the eight-hundredth time, he may finally become convinced that you won't cower to his will. Bravo! Nevertheless, he may try, in his exasperation, the following ploy: "Then how *long* will I have to keep playing this stupid instrument?"

Whatever you do, *don't* commit yourself to *any* time period, at least in front of the child. If you must answer something to limit further argument, try using the answer we always give in our household when one of our boys asks this inevitable question: "You can stop when you're eighteen." This is now a totally accepted edict in our family.

Just between you and me (and I hope my kids don't see this part of the book), we don't necessarily intend to hold them to this eighteen-year cut-off. A lot can happen between now and then; our youngest is only four at the time of this writing. By then, we might *want* to end music lessons for some of the positive reasons I mentioned above.

But in the meantime, this answer certainly saves a lot of arguments!

Making It Work for *You* —Try This:

1. How can you prevent your child's possible desire to quit his music lessons? Looking through the chapter headings in this book, try and determine if there are specific areas in which you could improve.

2. Ask yourself, "How well do I stand up under the persistent pressure of my child(ren)?" Recommit yourself to holding fast in those areas that you know are in their best interest.

3. If your child is asserting his desire to quit music, is he possibly voicing a legitimate need or problem that needs to be addressed? Trying hearing what is behind his words.

4. Talk to your child about perseverance, as well as the negative ramifications of being a quitter. Give them the football coach quote, and help them to see the long-term results of short-term toil.

Making It Work for You — It's True

1. Use a calm, pleasant tone of voice to calm down an upset child before I begin though the days goes past, I just look ahead and during the day you can just see it all working out along

2. I thought "I'll never make it" and I usually do, you never know "what day it" I never had my gueston so in we or ever different ones, as in the places, need to

3. I need to learn to show a more respect it is part of the hard. I learn to be calm, and I need to be patient. Since my guess when our lesson

Chapter Eleven

Breaking Through

◆ ◆ ◆

"How can I continue the motivation of a musical youth?"

I n the previous chapter, I dealt with the common problem
parents have in motivating a child who does not want to
continue in music. Now let's look at the other side of this
issue and examine an opposite but common situation.

"What does a parent (especially a non-musician parent) do
with a student who is *very* motivated musically?"

You may have a son or daughter who would rather play the
guitar than go to sleep. Many parents, after seeing their child
become self-motivated in music, might wonder if they have
created a monster. The child they brought into the world now
seems to live in his own world, and his young life is becoming
rather out of balance.

The last word of the previous sentence is the key word to
parenting such a musical child: balance!

BALANCE

Johann Sebastian Bach composed *The Well-Tempered
Clavier*. What we need is *The Well-Balanced Young Musician*.

How can parents help balance the busy lives of motivated young musicians? This is critically important, since our guidance today will shape the personal balancing of their lives tomorrow. To give some clarity, let us examine the two extremes of this issue:

In one house on your street is the *"pragmatic* parent"—often a father. When his son Timothy expresses his obsession with his trumpet, Dad gets mildly apprehensive. He loves his boy and wants to support this "little fancy," but he certainly doesn't want it to be taken seriously. After all, he has to "learn a trade" and "get on with the *real* world."

So he begins to limit his son's practice time. Timothy notices that there is a boring increase of lectures about making a living and providing for a family someday. Dad's influence can quickly escalate from subtle suggestion to overt opposition to Timothy's love of music.

I hope this warning will save many fathers a lot of worry: This type of approach never works. It tends to drive a painful wedge between parent and child, and usually encourages the student to become all the more faithful to his disparaged music. So we need to find a better way to deal with Timothy.

In another house on your street is the *"coddling* parent"—often a mother. When her daughter Sharon shows love for and talent with her flute, Mom's taxi service shifts into high gear. She becomes a single-minded chauffeur—lessons, rehearsals, concerts, master classes—patiently waiting in the car and comforting herself with thoughts of her daughter's first CD and debut performance at Carnegie Hall.

Meanwhile, Sharon is developing a rather distorted view of life. Everything begins to revolve around her—which, in fact, is now the truth. Her schoolwork suffers, but her mom says not to worry: "Stars don't need to know algebra." Nothing is allowed into the family that might interfere with her prodigy's budding career.

This method doesn't usually work either. If Sharon really does have the extraordinary talent to become a world-class musician—and *very* few children do—then she will turn into a self-important prima donna whom no one can stand. If she has merely enough talent to be a typical professional musician, Sharon will abruptly discover that, once she is away from Mom, no one will treat her like a star.

FINDING THE BALANCE

What is a good balance for a young motivated musician? On one hand, you should realize that to be an accomplished musician does require a great deal of effort, sacrifice, and time on the student's part. On the other hand, we want our children to be well-rounded, healthy, happy kids, not eccentric musical maniacs with swollen egos.

Scripture teaches the importance of being good stewards of the gifts God has given us. We want to teach our children how to offer their gifts back to God and to find the pivotal balance in their lives to achieve such stewardship.

Let's begin with three key guidelines for parents of musically motivated children:

1. Continue to confirm the importance of all the child's schoolwork. Your kids may love music, but they still must live in the real world. They may not like chemistry, but someday they will probably not like paying bills and doing their taxes. There are some things *all* of us simply must do.

Try to emphasize the importance of *all* learning, so that students see music as one of many branches of art and knowledge. In this way, they will not resent the time they must spend on these other subjects. Instead, they will see them as having the same value as their musical pursuits. Obviously, a great deal of their learning—from physics to English literature—will have a direct bearing on the study of music.

2. Help your child simplify her busy life. Kids in our society can find themselves very overcommitted. For many of them, saying "no" to something amusing is a slowly acquired practice. Almost all talented children need parental help in making "time choices" and in simplifying their lives.

Begin by helping Sally to sort out her activities into overall categories. Sit down with your daughter, pen and paper in hand, and examine her day-to-day activities. Every family is unique, so each child's categories will differ considerably. You might try to simplify Sally's life into the following four divisions:

A. Family obligations—These might include anything from daily chores to family meals, from church and her spiritual life to keeping her room presentable (or at least livable).

B. Schoolwork—This should only include what's on her report card, not the extracurricular activities. This category contains the indispensable schoolwork and homework of every student.

C. Music—This has now become a large slice of the pie. It may include lessons, practicing, performing, rehearsing, going to concerts, studying music (or music theory or music history), and listening to music.

D. All other possible activities—This will always be a huge part of anyone's life. But if she is serious about music, then Sally will have to learn to forego many of these items, especially if they are time-consuming but not very beneficial.

I'm not referring to eating and sleeping! I mean the thousands of diversions that take up Sally's time and cause the first three categories to suffer. Everything from the TV to long phone calls, from too many games to even the worthwhile activities after school. We all have exactly 24 hours to use each day. If Sally wants to spend a lot of time (and find a lot of great pleasure) in music, then she will probably need to say "no" to the smaller pleasure of these distractions.

3. Impress upon the child the importance of using the time devoted to her musical study *very* wisely. A good verse for your children to learn is Ephesians 5:15-16: "Be very careful, then, how you live—not as unwise but as wise, making the most of every opportunity."

Perhaps this is the key to any successful experience in music. The well-balanced musicians of any age are not those who deny themselves everything except music. Far from it! They are those who have learned to use their music time fruitfully, setting goals for themselves and accomplishing their musical tasks one day at a time.

Do you remember those powerful lines from Rudyard Kipling's poem "If"?

If you can fill the unforgiving minute,
With sixty seconds' worth of distance run,
Yours is the Earth and everything that's in it,
And—which is more—you'll be a Man, my son!

If only a student could always get sixty seconds' worth of quality practicing from every minute of practice time! That student would advance in a year far more than most do in four years. A young music student has much to learn in a relatively short amount of time. If he is going to find any satisfaction in his music, he needs to use his musical time wisely.

In short, motivated young musicians need to:

1. *Know what they should be doing.* That is, they need to know which of the various musical activities will propel them forward.

2. *Prioritize these different musical activities,* in the practical terms of "how much regular time should I allot to each possible activity."

3. *Do these things on a very regular basis,* refusing to allow the distractions of less-important activities interfere with their music

Let's review some of the many musical endeavors that will be found in the life of a music student. Some of these have already been covered in earlier chapters, but many contain new material for your motivated young musician.

INGREDIENTS OF A MUSICAL LIFE

These are not listed in any specific order; indeed, different singers and instrumentalists will need to establish their own order of priorities for such activities. They may also need to add other categories. But this list should help them begin.

Listening to music. This can be the perfect answer to time management problems. Kids can learn a vast number of pieces by playing music in the background of many other activities (not homework). This may be on selected CDs and tapes, or it could be through a nearby radio tuned to a good station.

This practice is very beneficial for the young musician but could wreak havoc in the family unless careful arrangements are made. Obviously, kids (and adults!) can disagree riotously over different musical styles they enjoy or detest. I hope you have more than one radio and tape player in the house. Closed doors and thick walls may come in handy, too.

Practicing. I have dedicated an entire chapter to this subject, so there's no need to belabor the point. In the words of the wise old New York cabbie who was asked by a lost country boy how to get to Carnegie Hall, "Practice, son, *practice!*"

Learning their repertoire. This is done in the practice room as well as by simply listening to music. But it is not the same as practicing that week's lesson or exercises. Take time to play through pieces that are considered standard repertoire, even if no performance is in sight. A good music teacher will list all of his student's standard literature for him.

This is critical if a student is considering a major in music at college. By the time a cellist, or a singer, or a clarinetist, arrives at music school, there are certain pieces he should already know, at least vaguely. The student should take the initiative himself and not wait for his teacher to assign these important works.

Lessons. Allow me to reiterate the supreme importance of private lessons already discussed in chapter six. To develop correct habits (both vocally and instrumentally), a student must avail himself of the expertise of a good teacher.

Rehearsing. I'm using this word in the plural sense. *Practicing* is what you do by yourself. *Rehearsing* is practicing music with others. Any musician in an ensemble—and all musicians should be!—will spend many hours in rehearsals.

There are essentially two kinds of rehearsals, and they require different types of involvement: the "conductor-led" rehearsal, and the "chamber music" rehearsal. For the former, the conductor has (hopefully) prepared the rehearsal agenda, and your part is to best respond to his leadership. In the conductor-less chamber music rehearsal, each player must initiate comments and bring out distinctive musical ideas.

Performing. It is the beautiful culmination of all a student has studied for. Not only does it demonstrate the combined skills of diligent practicing, but it is the sharing of one's musical experience with others. For more on this subject, go read chapter nine!

Going to concerts. In chapter 3 I discussed the idea of parents taking their young children to concerts. Now we will consider the many concerts that older kids will want to see for their own musical entertainment and inspiration.

Certainly, all violinists should go to violin concerts, all opera students should go to operas, and all bassoonists should go to bassoon concerts. But that's just the beginning. All students should attend a variety of performances, from orchestral to choral, from opera to chamber music. This is part of being a well-rounded musician.

Studying music. This is a category somewhere between listening to music and practicing new repertoire. By studying music I mean to sit down with a musical score in front of you, with or without a recording. The student learns to study the form, the style, the themes, the rhythm, and the harmonic content. Some of this will be supervised by the teacher, but much of it can be done privately by the student. This kind of keen musical analysis can be an invaluable preliminary to actually playing or singing a new piece of music.

Studying music history. Some students greatly undervalue this subject, either because they've been taught by boring teachers or because they don't really understand what music history is. The history of music is a fascinating subject. It is not a list of dates and cerebral facts. It tells the story of "what was behind" the music we love to play.

Perhaps the best place for young students to begin is by reading some of the excellent biographies of the great composers. They should select books on their favorite composers at a reading level to match their age and ability. Few things can better make the music come alive than to read about the life of the music's creators. (Some of these books are recommended in appendix 2, but dozens of other excellent ones are available at your public library. Ask your librarian to help you.)

Studying music theory. In the section concerning singers (Interlude Two), you learned about the importance of music theory in the education of a singer. But, of course, it is extremely important for instrumentalists as well and should never be taken for granted.

Many young musicians will say, "I don't know any music theory," when they actually know quite a bit. Indeed, if they can *read* music, they know some music theory. But if they are to learn the art of interpreting music, or if they ever want to teach music to others, they will need further study in this area. They must be able to analyze any piece of music on which they are working, to answer the essential question, "What is the composer trying to say?"

This is not very difficult and should not interfere with the ongoing study of their instrument. All good private teachers can teach enough music theory for young students, and will do so if asked. Furthermore, there are many excellent music theory books that a motivated student can read. For many young musicians, the knowledge needed can be acquired quickly once they realize the need for music theory in their education.

Master classes. For the motivated musician, a master class is a must. When a teacher near you (or a "star" who comes into town) announces a master class on your instrument or voice, sign up immediately. You need to be there.

There are usually two levels of participation. Advanced students sign up to play for the teacher and be critiqued before the entire assembly—which can be a rather nerve-racking ordeal. Or you can simply sign up to be in the audience, the "watchers," who will learn from observing the master working with the advanced students. Obviously, to be one of those who plays for a renowned teacher can be an event you'll never forget. But whether you're a performer or a watcher, participating in a master class is a fantastic musical experience.

Music camps. Here is another meaningful opportunity for musicians in junior high, senior high, and college. Each summer, music camps around the country are filled with thousands of students, where new and exciting musical experiences begin to happen. There are band camps, orchestra camps, opera camps, chamber music camps, choral camps, you name it!

This is the one time of year when a young musician can devote himself almost exclusively to his music, without the stress of the million extra pressures during the school year. These one-week to eight-week sessions are a perfect time to see if your kids want to consider music as a lifelong career. Whatever the result, it is also a fun time to meet dozens of new friends with similar aspirations. Sign your kids up today for a program near you next summer.

Competitions. Depending upon whom you talk to, music competitions are either the greatest experience for young musicians or the wretched bane of the musical art. Some musicians win competition after competition (sometimes including thousands of dollars!) and thereby launch a notable career. Others, perhaps equally talented, detest the nerve-racking atmosphere of competitions and refuse to consider entering one.

The realm of music competitions is vast. They range from local piano guild contests for youngsters to the famed Tchaikovsky International Music Competition held in Moscow. They can be either a blessing or a curse, depending on the disposition of your child. On one hand, competitions can provide tremendous motivation for your child to practice and excel, and a successful outcome makes it all worthwhile. On the other hand, they can give your child ulcers and sleepless nights, and an unsuccessful outcome can be devastating.

Therefore, know your children. Are they naturally competitive, racing to be the first in their class to finish and hand in a paper? Or do they get overwrought taking tests, perhaps doing poorly even when they know the material? Ponder these questions when you consider entering your child in a music competition. And let me know if your child ever wins the Tchaikovsky International!

Composition. Almost this entire book about musical kids assumes that they are performers (either instrumental or vocal), not *composers*. This is because all composers start as performers (playing someone else's compositions) and later begin to write their own material. Even the most gifted children seldom become serious composers until they are older, often well into college.

Nevertheless, how will they discover if composition is their gift unless they give it a try? All students should occasionally try to compose something that they will play or sing themselves. Not only will the results show any underlying compositional talent, but it will also help them as performers. To see things from the composer's point of view will certainly assist them as they endeavor to interpret the many pieces they will play or sing.

Such student compositions—instrumental or vocal—are usually done with the guidance of the private teacher. If your child Joey truly shows compositional aptitude, his teacher might want to direct him to a professional composer to further his specialized studies. Who knows? Joey might be the next Beethoven!

Music stores. If there is a young musician in your family, then you both need to know about your closest music stores.

Obviously, you will purchase many pieces of music there, but a good music store also has dozens of other musical accessories that will support your child's training and motivation. Sometime soon, go to the music store *without* your child and spend some time browsing to find out everything they have to offer. You would be amazed to find all that is available to encourage the education of young musicians. Once you are familiar with these various items, you may also want to check out the many excellent mail-order catalogues for musicians.

Music libraries. Likewise, you need to find the nearest music library. This will be in either a music school, the music department of the nearest university, or in the central library of a major city. A great education (for free!) is awaiting your musical child in this music library. This is where he can check out music, CDs, and hundreds of books, unless, of course, you would rather *buy* them all!

Meeting other musicians. Whatever other ventures you and your musical kids undertake, make certain to remember this: Musicians (of any age) need other musicians. They need to meet them, to talk with them, and, whenever possible, to work with them.

This is more than simply kids playing with other kids in various ensembles. Your child needs musical role models, leaders he can admire and emulate. Certainly, this is modeled by his teachers, but it should not stop there. Anytime a "star" is in your town, try to get them together, even for a few seconds for a handshake or an autograph. You'd be surprised at what an impact such a encounter can make on a young child.

As I've said throughout this book, to succeed in music a child needs more than to be taught: He needs to be *inspired*. He needs to be animated and infected with the joy of loving great music. What better means than to bring him into contact with those masters whose lives radiate this joy of music? In this way they too can catch the vision, and such inspiration can get them through many hours of toil in the practice room.

When Beethoven was a young man—a talented but unknown pianist—he was brought before the great, renowned Mozart, who was then recognized as one of the world's greatest musicians. After hearing him play, Mozart turned to one of his friends and uttered a prophetic remark: "Keep your eyes on him. Someday he will give the world something to talk about." Doubtless such a comment must have been quite an encouragement for the young Beethoven—it certainly brought results! Now, how about *your* young musician?

Making It Work for *You* —Try This:

1. Examine your present attitude about helping your child's music experience. Are you the "pragmatic parent," the "coddling parent"—or somewhere in between?

2. Talk to your musical children about the balance (or lack of balance) in their lives. Help them to simplify their lives, dividing their time into such categories as "family obligations," "schoolwork," and "musical activities."

3. Go through the "ingredients of a musical life" with your kids. What sections are important to them? Is enough time regularly allotted for these essential categories? Remember, we are *always* seeking to FIND THE BALANCE.

Chapter Twelve

Looking Down
the Road

◆ ◆ ◆

"Should my child spend his or her life in music?"

My wife knew from the ninth grade that she wanted to spend her life in music; the scholarships she obtained to go to music school merely confirmed what she already knew. For those who started music at an early age and have long enjoyed the success of their talents, the decision to devote their lives to music is an easy one.

But for many who have spent years taking music lessons or performing in school, the decision of whether to major in music or go to music school can be especially difficult. Perhaps no other subject (such as business, medicine, or law) seems an obvious choice for them. Perhaps they have enjoyed their musical experiences but have no idea how they would fare in the "real world" of musical competition.

I have seen many young students agonize over this issue. Over the years many parents have talked to me about these questions. They have prayed, sought counsel, and talked hours with their son or daughter, yet are often without clear answers. After teaching in both high schools and colleges, I have come to a number of basic conclusions about which types of students will or will not prosper as music majors.

Statistics tell us that a very small percentage of performers who graduate with music degrees will earn a living performing on their instruments, even ten years later. While learning music is in itself a good thing, such statistics are still alarming to someone considering a music major.

To simplify this issue, I want to discuss three critical elements that every successful musician must have. If your child is to successfully major in music he should possess a large allotment of three ingredients: talent, discipline, and what I call the musician's "devotion."

TALENT

A student should have a great deal of musical talent if he is even considering a music major in college. One might think that this is obvious. Yet any music professor will tell you that there are students in his department who really should be pursuing other careers because they lack the talent necessary for a successful career in music. How does this happen?

To begin with, it is rather uncomfortable for a music teacher to tell his high school student (or even the student's parents) that the student is not very talented, and therefore shouldn't major in music. So the less-talented student is naively "passed upstairs" to a music department that badly needs tuition income (they all do) and has often lowered its entrance standards to the point of accepting *anyone* who has the money to pay. This unfortunately happens every year across the country.

I have actually seen freshmen show up at music school who don't even know how to *read music!* This unsuspecting student soon finds himself sitting next to musicians who have already been performing for over a decade. It is almost like sending someone who is illiterate to major in English literature.

What is the answer to this awkward situation? Parents must take the initiative while their children are still in high school. They need to talk privately to the music teachers and exact an honest answer to the question, "Is my child *really* talented enough that he or she should major in music?" By the time a music student is a high school senior, it is usually obvious to the musically discerning whether or not that student has what it takes.

Unfortunately, many parents don't want to actually ask such a question because they don't want to hear a negative answer. They would rather live in a fantasy world, dreaming of their child performing concerti with the world's major orchestras. But as painful as it may be, it is far better to find out the talent level early on than to spend thousands of dollars and years of wasted effort for a student who never should have majored in music at all.

To send a less-talented student to major in music is to subject him to frustration (in his studies), scorn (by the talented students), and unrealistic expectations (that someday he will see his name in lights). The music profession is unbelievably competitive, and getting more so every year. The only students who have even a small chance of "making it"—that is, having a successful profession in music—are those with a considerable amount of talent, preparation, and experience when they enter the college level.

Before sending your child off to a music department, make sure that he truly has the talent for it. *Never* simply rely on one source, such as the student's private teacher. You should arrange to have your child meet several musical authorities, college-level music teachers, and professional musicians. The student should perform for them, and discuss music until the depth of his musical knowledge is clear to the expert.

Afterward, the parent should talk privately to these unbiased experts and base decisions and plans on their objective advice.

SELF-DISCIPLINE

Through the years I have known many musicians who were so musically gifted that they could have done almost anything, yet they never excelled. Why? Because of a lack of internal discipline, an unwillingness to commit the necessary time and effort for the pursuit of excellence in their field. *No one* is so talented that all music is immediately easy. Indeed, some music is so challenging that even musicians of the highest caliber must spend many years in solitary practice to master it.

There is simply no substitute for discipline and hard work. "All hard work brings a profit," King Solomon wrote, "but mere talk leads only to poverty" (Prv 14:23). The advice he gave in Ecclesiates might have been written specifically for young musicians: "Whatever your hand finds to do, do it with all your might" (Ecc 9:10).

Of course, as we've discussed earlier in this book, discipline is important for learning music at every stage. But when a student goes off to college to major in music, two new factors come into play:

The first has to do with the greater degree of peer competition the student meets as a freshman. Even though your violinist daughter Rebbecah played with many peers in her high school orchestra, she was also surrounded by dozens of friends who were not musicians. Now she suddenly finds herself in an environment almost devoid of non-musicians, and many of her classmates are *very* talented. She quickly realizes that the only ones who have a good chance of succeeding are those who are giving it everything they have.

A second factor that enters a freshman's life has to do with the need for *self-discipline*. By this time in a music student's life, one's discipline must be completely internal to be successful. There can no longer exist a need for such external motivation as parental supervision or the constant encouragement of a teacher.

When a student is young, parents enforce practicing and teachers reward every effort with praise and encouragement. In music school, parents aren't usually nearby. If internal discipline hasn't become an ingrained habit by now, practicing becomes irregular, grades slip, and skills become slipshod. Teachers typically have too many students to be able to heap encouragement on every newcomer, and many freshman musicians never make it to their sophomore year.

The cause of musical "dropouts" is not always a lack of talent but often a lack of self-discipline. No student should major in music unless he is ready, willing, and able to start his practicing early and finish it late—and without any outside motivation. The musicians who thrive in college are those who put in extra hours of work without anyone's notice or approval. They do it because *they* want to do it.

THE MUSICIAN'S "DEVOTION"

This section may raise a few eyebrows, but it is essential. There are some students who are very talented and even very disciplined, yet they do not achieve distinction in music. There are even a few musicians who, because of their enormous talent and discipline, reach a level of distinction in music—yet are not happy or fulfilled in their success. This problem has to do with a lack of what I call the musician's devotion.

By the word "devotion," I am not referring to anyone's personality or to character traits. Musicians, like any other group of people, come in all types, with an infinite variety of likes and dislikes. Their personalities may be flamboyant or serene, gregarious or withdrawn. Some are well read and intellectually brilliant; others seem to have musical talent exclusively. This is not the area of demeanor I am addressing.

What I mean by the musician's devotion has to do with the manner in which he or she ultimately regards music itself. When I'm with a young musician, some of the questions I like to ask are:

"How much do you really love music itself?"

"You are going to be spending thousands of hours by yourself practicing music that few besides yourself will ever hear; *why* would you want to do such a thing?"

"What are your fundamental reasons and motives for playing (or singing) music?"

These are penetrating questions that may make us rather uncomfortable. Yet such thoughts are necessary because they bring to light an essential element for anyone who is considering a lifetime in music.

From a purely pragmatic point of view, a musical career can be *very* hard. It isn't a nine-to-five job that can simply be turned off at the end of the day. It means long, thankless hours in the practice room, with little monetary reward or public acclamation. Even those in the top echelons of musical success, such as those in a professional orchestra or teachers in a top conservatory, do not make the opulent salaries of those at the top in such fields as banking, law, or many other occupations.

The bottom line is, if you are going to be happy in the world of music, then you had better *love music* very much to begin with—otherwise, you may be rather disappointed.

It is this indispensable love of the music itself—not what practical rewards it can bring you—that is the essence of what I have called the musician's devotion.

It is what keeps a great student playing for hours in a small practice room, long after his personal discipline has run out.

He loves the music itself; it is self-rewarding, even as it is still being perfected. The finished product, perhaps a public performance, is only what the outside world sees. The real love was evident back in the lonely practice room.

Even those who believe that God is calling them to a life in music should carefully and prayerfully consider this matter. It is part of "counting the cost" that we are admonished to do before undertaking any great endeavor (see Luke 14:26-35). An honest appraisal of one's situation may save many years of regrets.

I once knew a performer who was incredibly talented and disciplined. This girl was so extraordinary that by her sophomore year in college, she was already performing with one of the world's top orchestras, and everyone predicted a tremendously successful career in music.

To everyone's utter astonishment, she soon quit music entirely and eventually went to law school. After many more years starting over in classes where everyone was a decade younger than she, this musical prodigy had a rather normal architecture career—but was much happier and fulfilled as a person.

Why? What happened to her meteoric climb as a professional musician? This girl never really *loved* the music she was playing every day. She was so gifted that for years everyone told her that she could go to the top, but no one ever asked her the simple questions I mentioned above. She never had this musician's devotion, and when this finally dawned upon her, she had to take some rather drastic action to find her true fulfillment in life.

Reviewing the three essential elements of talent, discipline, and devotion, I conclude: Everyone knows that talent is needed, and most can see that self-discipline is also an important element. But the need for this last factor is often overlooked, to the student's detriment. Before we send our children off to music school, let's explore the whole person and make certain that the inherent love of music itself is a part of their devotion.

FINDING THE RIGHT MUSIC SCHOOL

By the generic term "music school," I simply mean a department of music within a college or university, or a music conservatory. The technical differences between such institutions are not important at this point. For now, I am concerned with helping parents select a musical establishment that is best suited for their son or daughter who wants to major in music.

There are many practical factors in selecting a specific music school. Cost and location are obviously two of the predominant determinants. I do not know how much you can personally afford, nor do I know whether you insist that your child go to college nearby or are open to more distant locations. I want to advise you in the broader determinants that all students face.

For performers the most important rule to follow is: don't look for the best music school, look for the best *teacher*. A student may get into a music school with a famous reputation, but if he can't stand the principal teacher he will be working with, he is in big trouble. The problem is very common, especially with people who look only for the big-name schools.

To begin with, remember that learning music is not primarily a classroom experience. It is best communicated one-to-one. Furthermore, even the finest music schools have some departments that may be second-rate. One school may have a world-class piano department, but its composition department could be seriously deficient. Whatever the school's overall reputation, a composition major could be very disappointed and frustrated in such a school.

So it is best to know the key individual(s) that the student will be working with before applying to specific music schools. This "key individual" principle also follows for non-performers, those who will be working on a degree in music education, composition, or musicology. In these cases, the key individual you need to know is usually the director of your specific department. Generally, the spirit of a music ed department or a musicology department will clearly reflect the spirit of its leader. Good rapport with the primary director is essential.

Therefore, in the years before college, students need to meet with college teachers who may potentially be their primary teacher or department head one day. Obviously, their present teachers will have to guide them toward the right people, since their teachers will know the musical "who's who" that the student needs to meet. This practice may seem difficult and even expensive at the time, but its rewards will be abundant once the student is in college. It can mean the difference between a fruitful, fulfilling time at college and a miserable period of frustration and disappointment.

A word of caution to performers: In selecting your music school using this "key person" principle, be careful if you pick a big-name teacher or performer with which to study. Even if you are accepted at a school where a "Horowitz" teaches, you may only see your Horowitz once every few months—and find yourself studying with a graduate student most of the time, whom you may or may not like. You would be wiser to make your selection based on that person whom you will be working with the most.

WHAT ABOUT DIFFERENT TYPES OF MUSIC MAJORS?

At one time, if you were an oboist and you went to music school, you undoubtedly became an "oboe major." That is, you worked toward a degree in music performance with oboe as your principal instrument. This is often called "applied music performance." In earlier centuries, music schools offered two basic paths: one for performers and one for composers.

Today there are many more options. Entire books have been written on this baffling subject due to the expansion of music departments and the multitudinous "major in/minor in" alternatives at many colleges and universities. Within the music department it is common to, for example, major in composition and minor in conducting. And throughout colleges today, you may even run into someone who is majoring in oboe but minoring in chemistry, or majoring in psychology but minoring in music therapy!

Let's simplify a bit for the sake of clarity. The basic music programs at most schools in which students can major include performance (on every classical instrument), conducting, composition, musicology (or music history), music theory, and music education. Many schools also offer such majors as music therapy, recording, or electronic music, but these are usually approached by students coming from the traditional majors.

Obviously, if a high school student is determined to be a composer and has demonstrated ability in this area, he will want to major in composition (though he will still need a "major instrument," which may or may not be piano). If your daughter Sarah is crazy about the study of music history, she will probably go for a musicology degree.

"PERFORMANCE" OR "MUSIC EDUCATION," THAT IS THE QUESTION

Other situations are not so definite. Surely the greatest question in the minds of many young musicians (and their parents) is: "Should I be a performance major or go into music education?"

What many of them are really saying with this question is:

"I'd love to play my instrument professionally, but I don't know if I'll make the grade. Therefore, maybe I should play it safe by majoring in music education so that I'll at least be able to get a job teaching someday."

This is the wrong kind of thinking. Having been a professional musician for many years—and not a rich one—I can easily sympathize with financial fears. But I have known dozens of great music educators and dozens of great performers, and their respective professions are too honorable to abuse with such wrong thinking.

First of all, the schools of this country need great music educators, *not* mediocre performers who just *want a job*. Such second-choice education majors usually make horrible teachers and will later have the opportunity to ruin a generation of would-be music lovers.

You should go into music education *because you want to be an outstanding teacher*, because you are called to the noble teaching profession and will inspire your future students to love and appreciate music as you do. *No one* should enter education for the negative reasons of insecurity as a performer or financial trepidation.

Almost all performers teach, either privately or at schools. Generally, performers privately teach their specific instruments, while music educators teach in a wide variety of settings from classrooms of students in general music to chorus, band, and string ensembles. But there are many exceptions for both professions.

Thousands with performance degrees have teaching jobs, and for that matter, thousands of teachers are also excellent performers. If you specifically want to teach in certain public school districts, then you will probably need to be certified with specific music education requirements. Adjustments in curriculum can be dealt with later than as a freshman entering music school. After a few years in college, one's career choices become more apparent. If changes are needed in your degree program, there is still plenty of time.

To sum up: Become a music education major if you love to teach and want to teach. Become a performance major if you love your instrument and want to play your instrument. Later on, with more experience, if you feel like you want to change majors, it's not difficult. But let's start out with the right principle.

APPLY EVERYWHERE THAT LOOKS PLAUSIBLE

As you can see from the "finding the key teacher" principle I discussed earlier, going to music school is not like majoring in most non-musical subjects. Usually, if students decide to major in engineering or computer science, they simply apply to the nearest state college (also the least expensive), get their degree in four years and get a nice nine-to-five job in their field.

The music world is not quite that simple. Your local state college may have a small music department with few teachers with whom you would like to study. To find your best "key teacher" you may have to look further than the nearest state college. Since this can get expensive, the need for music scholarships becomes a major consideration.

Many books have been written on the subject of obtaining scholarships, and you should probably buy a few and read them thoroughly. As I've already mentioned, music scholarships are not always given based on performance skill alone. Rather, they often result from the need of that specific music department. This is why an outstanding flutist may be turned down, and the scholarship given to a less outstanding violinist—the college needs many violinists in its orchestra.

Therefore, the best rule is to apply to a number of different music schools where you would feel comfortable. Performers should take every audition they can set up; the experience itself is good, and it prepares you for the time when a good audition can be a lifetime turning point.

Unless you are wealthy, you should always apply for scholarships. Even if you don't expect to get one, it doesn't hurt to ask. Once, while applying for a scholarship, I happened to check a little box on the application that meant I might also be considered for a fellowship (no tuition, plus a stipend!). Imagine my delight when I won both and got to choose. You may be pleasantly surprised by such an award, and it can be a deciding factor in your final choice of music schools.

Making It Work for *You* —Try This:

1. TALK to your child—*A LOT*—about his future. How does he really feel about music? (Explore the other questions given in this chapter.)

2. Talk to your child about talent, discipline, and the musician's devotion. How strongly does he rate himself in these areas?

3. Talk to your child's music teacher(s), especially about these three areas. Ask other musical experts about your child's future.

4. Investigate a few prospective music schools, and make it a point to talk to their faculties. If possible, take your child into that environment for a day or so. Is he comfortable? Is this in his future?

Conclusion

◆ ◆ ◆

Music for a Lifetime

Before we drive away from the music school and leave our sons and daughters behind, let's ask one more question. Is their purpose to become professional musicians or fulfilled music-lovers?

Earlier I mentioned that the majority of performers who graduate with music degrees do not go on to have long-term careers in music. The laws of supply-and-demand are against them. There are not enough music jobs for all the music graduates. Therefore, many musicians become secretaries, executives, computer experts, doctors, ministers, lawyers, postmen, journalists, and politicians.

You may think this is rather sad, and in some ways it is. Yet even for those who do not have a music career, the music school experience is a positive one that will stay with them for a lifetime. Even if your son Bob works through four years of college music only to later become a computer hacker, those years will never be considered a waste.

Ask yourself: Which is better, a computer hacker with no

appreciation for music, or a computer hacker who—largely due to years of music study—will always have a deep love for music? Bob may continue to play in amateur groups, and will be one of the most faithful fans of the local symphony and opera company.

I was once discussing this with Luis Haza, who is a violinist in the National Symphony and also the conductor of the American Youth Orchestra—one of the finest in the world. He told of the hundreds of kids who played the great symphonies in his youth orchestra, yet who chose not to become professional musicians. Yet those wonderful memories would remain. Your son, Bob, may make this choice one day. But for the rest of his music-loving life, every time Bob goes to a concert of a great symphony he played as a child, that youthful exhilaration will return to him again.

Furthermore, Bob's love for music will surely be passed on to his children. Little Bob, Jr. will hear music from the earliest ages and will soon discover the joy of music from his parent's experience. Indeed, with the support of his father, Bob, Jr. might be the next Horowitz. And if not, he will live a life of greater happiness and fulfillment because of his love of music—passing it on again to the next generation.

In the introduction to this book, I said that not all of us have a little Mozart for a child. But how about one for a grandchild someday, or maybe a great-grandchild! When you take the time and effort to open the world of music for your child, it's impossible to predict how far this inspiration may influence him. Those little piano lessons you're paying for may be the beginning of the next Bach dynasty of musicians.

Lest you think that this is farfetched, let me illustrate from history the power of a parent's musical influence. It is astonishing to find how many of history's greatest musicians were born to parents who were themselves amateur musicians or music lovers.

MUSIC TREK... THE NEXT GENERATION

Beethoven's father was a singer in the Electoral Chapel in Bonn. His grandfather also was a singer. Bizet's dad was a vocal teacher, and Offenbach's was the cantor at the Cologne Synagogue. Stravinsky's father was even a leading bass singer at the St. Petersburg opera.

It is astonishing to see how many composer's mothers played the piano—sometimes professionally, sometimes as keyboard-loving amateurs. The list includes such masters as Grieg, Britten, de Falla, Honegger, Mussorgsky, Scriabin, and Rachmaninoff. Two notables whose fathers played piano are Rimsky-Korsakov and Liszt—the latter becoming the greatest pianist of his century!

String players often seem to beget great composers. Those with a violinist for a father include Mozart, Smetana, von Weber, and Vivaldi. Composers who grew up listening to their fathers playing the cello include Schubert, Dohnanyi, and Villa-Lobos. Brahms' father played the double bass in the municipal theater in Hamburg.

Some composers even had mothers and fathers who played music. Both Chopin and Rossini had mothers who were excellent singers, but Chopin's father played the flute and Rossini's father the horn. Both of Shostakovich's parents were pianists and had to take turns practicing—only to have the schedule further complicated when their son also began to practice. Walton's parents were both singing teachers, and his father the choirmaster of a local church.

Other composers grew up in church rehearsals because their fathers were organists. The most notable are Elgar (whose father also played violin and operated a music store) and Puccini (who came from three generations of musicians). Speaking of musical generations, how about Bach? Practically his entire family tree was musical. Over fifty musicians bearing that name are remembered by musicologists today.

The list goes on and on, from Richard Strauss' very professional father (he played first horn in the Munich Orchestra) to Haydn's very nonprofessional father (he played harp in his living room). Whether the parent was playing for fun or for a living, all of these succeeded in inspiring the next generation to love great music.

CARE TO BEGIN A NEW MUSICAL DYNASTY?

Of course, you don't have to be a musician to inspire your sons or daughters. Some of history's greatest composers—including such masters as Mendelssohn, Verdi, Franck, Paganini, and many others—came from parents who were not musicians themselves. Yet the care and support these parents gave their talented children resulted in a wealth of music that has blessed millions of listeners for many decades.

What about you? Whether you know nothing about music or are a professional musician, you can give the gift of great music to your children. And they to their children, and on and on. Who knows? Perhaps musicologists someday will be studying the many renowned musicians who bear your last name. Or perhaps your gift to your children will simply succeed in bringing a little more joy into their lives. Either way, it's wonderful.

Epilogue

◆ ◆ ◆

Handel's Dad

I conclude with a stark contrast. In this book's introduction I mentioned the large role that Mozart's father played in his son's success as a musician. His father found the best teachers available, enforced many hours of practice, and even arranged for performances all over Europe. He simply loved to show off his marvelous son, and they both benefited from the outcome.

In contrast, let's look at one of history's most notorious music-haters, the father of George Frideric Handel. This man opposed any musical inclinations in his son because he considered music-loving a sign of weakness! Handel's sympathetic mother helped him smuggle a spinet into the attic, covering the strings with strips of cloth so that his father wouldn't hear him practicing.

The only reason Handel's father ever let the boy take lessons was because of the pressure from his boss, the local duke. After recognizing Handel's tremendous talent, the Elector of Brandenburg was so impressed that he offered to finance Handel's intensive musical study in Italy—his father said, "Forget it." He considered a career in music out of the question and insisted that his musical genius go to law school at the University of Halle.

The result? Well, his father soon died, so Handel's musical career became unhindered. He was given fabulous offers, studied abroad, and eventually composed some of history's finest music. But his father never lived to see his son become the most renowned composer of his day, creating such a timeless masterpiece as *Messiah*, with its ever-popular "Hallelujah Chorus."

Indeed, had his father lived a few more decades, Handel's musical career would never have happened, and we would certainly never have heard of him or of the music that he later composed. A rather sad thought.

I wish every parent in the world could hear this story. Obviously, we don't all have Handels as children, but many of us might. Let's find out. Let's take the time, effort, and expense to discover what talents our children may have. Whether another Handel is discovered or not, your children's lives will forever be enhanced by the love, joy, and inspiration of great music.

Appendix One

◆ ◆ ◆

Great Music for Kids to Hear

For years people have asked me to recommend specific pieces of music that their children might like to hear. Since my personal field of expertise is that of classical music, the following list of pieces represents a broad spectrum of classical compositions that have exceptional appeal to the young, inexperienced listener. Unlike many works that may take time to appreciate, these pieces are fun to hear *the very first time*.

Obviously, every child is different, and what one child likes to hear may not please another child. Yet there are some universal qualities that tend to fascinate children, even at the first listening. These include such general characterizations as *fast, loud, lots of contrast, and much orchestral color*.

Therefore, you will notice that the majority of the works listed below are for orchestra. Kids of all ages are especially enchanted with the huge array of sound created by a full orchestra. Of course, there are other genres represented in the following list, particularly that of solo piano. But if you want to turn a youth on to music, there is no substitute for the orchestra. Its colorful combination of dozens of instruments makes it generally the best place to begin.

There is also the idea of "excerpts." Many pieces contain a *portion* that all kids love, but which may be preceded or followed by long sections that have less immediate appeal. But, of course, we want them to learn to appreciate the entirety of a composition and not merely to hear one short fragment after another. Besides, this would be rather difficult. It is not a practical solution to point out such details as "the best part your kids will like in the Debussy *Nocturnes* is found in measures 116 to 173 in the second movement!"

To address this situation, I have taken a middle course. Since many of these recommendations have multiple movements, I have suggested the best *movement* to play for your child. If you want to play the entire composition for him, fine. But in all probability, he will be initially interested in the recommended movement.

Certainly, you should *not* feel like your child needs to hear *every* piece on this list. Nor is it exclusive; there are doubtless other works that your child may enjoy instantly. But this list is given to help you begin. Take it to your local CD store and see what you can find. Enjoy!

BACH
  Brandenberg Concerto No. 2, Third Mvt.
  Brandenberg Concerto No. 4, First Mvt.
  Italian Concerto, Last Mvt.
  Fugue in G Minor "The Little"
  French Suite No. 5 in G Major
  Gavotte
  Gigue
  Cantata No. 147, Choral Prelude: "Jesu, Joy of Man's Desiring"
  Suite No. 2 in B Minor for Flute and Strings
  Rondeau
  Toccata and Fugue in D Minor

BARTOK
  Mikrokosmos

Hungarian Sketches, Evening in the Village
Concerto for Orchestra, Last Mvt.

BEETHOVEN
Minuet in G
Symphony No. 1, Third Mvt.
Symphony No. 5, First Mvt.
Symphony No. 6, First Mvt.
Symphony No. 9, Fourth Mvt.
Violin Concerto, Last Mvt.
Für Elise

BERLIOZ
Roman Carnival Overture

BERNSTEIN
Candide Overture

BIZET
L'Arlesienne Suite No. 2
Carillon
Farandole
Minuetto
Carmen Prelude, Act I
Children's Games
Soap Bubbles
The Top

BRAHMS
Symphony No. 4, Third Mvt.
Concerto for Violin and Cello, Last Mvt.
Cradle Song
Hungarian Dance No. 5

BRITTEN
Simple Symphony, Playful Pizzicato
Serenade, Prologue
** *The Young Person's Guide to the Orchestra*
A Ceremony of Carols, Welcome Yule!

BRUCH
Scottish Fantasy for Violin and Orchestra

CHOPIN
Etude in E Minor, Op. 25, No. 5
Polonaise in A Major, Op. 40, No. 1
Prelude in C-Sharp Minor, Op. 28, No. 10
Waltz, Op. 64, No. 1 "Minute Waltz"

COPLAND
The Red Pony, Circus Music
Rodeo, Hoedown
Twelve Poems of Emily Dickinson
Old American Songs
Billy the Kid, Street in a Frontier Town
Appalachian Spring, Variations on Simple Gifts

DEBUSSY
Nocturnes, Second Mvt.
Iberia, Last Mvt.
Children's Corner Suite
Jimbo's Lullaby
The Snow Is Dancing
Gardens in the Rain
Pagodes
La Mer, Play of the Waves
Syrinx, for Unaccompanied Flute
String Quartet, Second Mvt.
Preludes, Book 1, Voiles

DOWLAND
Come Again

DVORAK
Slavonic Dance, Op. 46, No. 1
Symphony No. 6, Third Mvt.
Symphony No. 9, Third Mvt.
String Quartet in F "American," Last Mvt.
Humoresque, Op. 101

FAURE
Dolly Suite, Berceuse
Requiem, Pie Jesu

GLIERE
The Red Poppy, Russian Sailor's Dance

GRIEG
Peer Gynt Suite No. 1
Anitra's Dance
Ase's Death
In the Hall of the Mountain King
Concerto in A Minor, First Mvt.

GROFE
Grand Canyon Suite, Cloudburst
Death Valley Suite, Desert Water Hole
Grand Canyon Suite, On the Trail

HANDEL
Solomon, Arrival of the Queen of Sheba
Music for the Royal Fireworks
Bouree
Minuet
Messiah, Hallelujah Chorus
The Harmonious Blacksmith
Water Music, Hornpipe

HAYDN
Symphony No. 45 "Farewell," Last Mvt.
Symphony No. 94 "Surprise," Second Mvt.
Cello Concerto No. 2 in D Major, Last Mvt.
Divertimento in E Flat, Echo, Hob.II:39

HOLST
The Planets, Mars

HONEGGER
King David, March of the Philistines
Pacific 231

HUMPERDINCK
  Hansel and Gretel
  Brother, Come and Dance with Me
  Nibble, Nibble, Mousekin
  Prayer
  Prelude
  Susie, Little Susie
  Tra-la-la-la

IBERT
  Divertissement, Parade

IVES
  Three Places in New England, Putnam's Camp, Redding,
    Connecticut
  Variations on "America"

KABALEVSKY
  Twenty-Four Pieces for Children, A Sad Story
  The Comedians, Pantomime

KODALY
  Hary Janos Suite, The Viennese Musical Clock

MENDELSSOHN
  A Midsummer Night's Dream, Scherzo
  Symphony No. 4 "Italian," Last Mvt.

MEYERBEER
  Waltz from Les Patineurs

MOZART
  Symphony No. 40, First Mvt.
  Symphony No. 41 "Jupiter," Last Mvt.
  A Little Night Music, First and Fourth Mvts.
  Horn Concerto No. 4, Last Mvt.
  Clarinet Concerto in A Major, Last Mvt.
  Adagio for Glass Harmonica
  Quintet for Clarinet and Strings in A Major,
    Fourth Mvt.
  Rondo "alla Turca"

The Sleigh Ride
Variations on "Ah, vous dirai-je, Maman"

MUSSORGSKY
Pictures at an Exhibition
Ballet of the Unhatched Chicks
Promenade
The Old Castle

OFFENBACH
Tales of Hoffman, Barcarolle

PACHELBEL
Canon

PROKOFIEV
Classical Symphony, First Mvt.
Love for Three Oranges, March
Summer Day Suite, March
Winter Bonfire, Departure
** *Peter and the Wolf*
Lieutenant Kije Suite:
  The Birth of Kije
  The Wedding of Kije
  Troika

PUCCINI
Madame Butterfly, Un abel di vedremo

PURCELL
The Indian Queen, Entrada
Trumpet Tune in D Major

RAVEL
Le Tombeau de Couperin, Minuet
Mother Goose Suite
Conversations of Beauty and the Beast
Laideronette, Empress of the Pagodas
String Quartet in F, Last Mvt.
Daphnis and Chloe, Suite No. 2
Bolero

RESPIGHI
> *The Pines of Rome,* Last Mvt.
> *Ancient Airs and Dances, Suite No. 2,* Last Mvt.

RIMSKY-KORSAKOV
> *Scheherazade,* First Mvt.
> *Russian Easter Overture*
> *The Tale of Tsar Sultan,* Flight of the Bumblebee

RODRIGO
> *Concierto de Aranjuez,* First Mvt.

ROSSINI
> *The Thieving Magpie Overture*
> *William Tell Overture*

SAINT-SAENS
> **Carnival of the Animals*

SCARLATTI
> *Sonata in G Minor,* K.30(L. 499) Cat Fugue

SCHUBERT
> *Symphony No. 8* "Unfinished," First Mvt.
> *Symphony No. 9* "The Great," Third Mvt.
> *String Quartet No. 14,* Last Mvt: Death & the Maiden
> *The Erlking*
> *March Militaire No. 1*
> *Four Ecossaises,* No. 1

SCHUMANN
> *Album for the Young,* Book 1
> The Happy Farmer
> Soldiers' March
> The Wild Horseman
> *Scenes from Childhood,* Dreaming

SHOSTAKOVICH
> *The Age of Gold,* Polka

SIBELIUS
> *Karelia Suite,* Alla Marcia
> *Finlandia*

SMETANA
Ma Vlast, The Moldau
The Bartered Bride Overture

STRAUSS, RICHARD
Till Eulenspiegel's Merry Pranks

STRAVINSKY
The Firebird:
  Berceuse
  Infernal Dance
Petrushka:
  Coachmen's Dance
  Russian Dance
Symphony of Psalms, First Mvt.
Pulcinella Suite, Tarantella

TCHAIKOVSKY
  ** *The Nutcracker*
Album for the Young, March of the Tin
  Soldiers
Symphony No. 4, Fourth Mvt.
Symphony No. 6 "Pathetique," Third Mvt.
Romeo & Juliet Overture
1812 Overture
Marche Slav
Sleeping Beauty
Swan Lake

VAUGHAN WILLIAMS
Fantasia on "Greensleeves"
Mass in G Minor, Kyrie
Folk Song Suite, March

VILLA-LOBOS
Bachianas Brasileiras No. 2, The Little Train of the Caipira

VIVALDI
Concerto for Guitar D Major, Third Mvt.
The Four Seasons, Winter

WAGNER
The Flying Dutchman Overture
Tannhauser Overture
The Mastersinger Overture
Lohengrin Overture
The Ring of the Nibelungen, Ride of the Valkyries

WEBERN
Eight Fragments, Three Pieces

** These compositions are the "Top Four" of all time for children. Every movement of each is a must!

Appendix Two:

◆ ◆ ◆

Recommended Music Books for Parents and Kids

For parents who want more information in specific musical areas, the following books are recommended:

INTRODUCTORY MUSIC BOOKS

Bernstein, Leonard. *The Joy of Music.* New York: Simon & Schuster, 1959.

Copland, Aaron. *What to Listen for in Music.* rev. ed. New York: McGraw-Hill, 1957.

Dallin, L. *Listener's Guide to Musical Understanding.* Dubuque, Iowa: W. C. Brown, 1977.

Kavanaugh, Patrick. *A Taste for the Classics.* Nashville, Tenn.: Sparrow Press, 1993.

Machlis, Joseph. *The Enjoyment of Music.* 3rd ed. New York: Norton, 1970.

MUSIC BOOKS FOR PARENTS

Ben-Tovim, Atarah, and Douglas Boyd. *The Right Instrument for Your Child: Practical Guide for Parents and Teachers.* New York: William Morrow and Company, 1985.

Bloom, Benjamin. *Developing Talent in Young People.* New York: Ballantine Books, 1985.

GENERAL MUSIC BOOKS

Headington, Christopher. *History of Western Music.* New York: Schirmer Books, 1976.

Hoffer, Charles R. *The Understanding of Music.* Belmont, Calif.: Wadsworth Publishing, 1968.

Machlis, Joseph. *The Enjoyment of Music.* 5th ed. New York: Norton and Company, 1984.

Stolba, K. Marie. *The Development of Western Music: A History.* Dubuque, Iowa: Wm. C. Brown, 1990.

Ulrich, Homer. *Music: A Design for Listening.* 3rd ed. New York: Harcourt, Braw and World, 1970.

MUSIC REFERENCE BOOKS

Ammer, Christine. *Harper's Dictionary of Music.* New York: Barnes and Noble, 1972.

Apel, Willi. *Harvard Dictionary of Music.* Cambridge: Harvard University Press, 1987.

Barlow, H. and S. Morgenstern. *A Dictionary of Musical Themes.* New York: Crown, 1948.

Duckles, V. *Music Reference and Research Materials: Bibliography.* New York: Free Press, 1974.

Fling, R. M., ed. *A Basic Music Library: Essential Scores and Books.* Chicago, Ill.: American Library Association, 1983.

Grammand, P. *The Harmony Illustrated Encyclopedia of Classical Music.* New York: Harmony Books, 1988.

Grove, Sir George, ed. *Grove's Dictionary of Music and Musicians.* 9 vols. New York: St. Martin's, 1954.

Hindley, G. *The Larousse Encyclopedia of Music.* New York: Word Publishing, 1971.

Pallay, S. G. *Cross-Index Title Guide to Classical Music.* Westport, Conn.: Greenwood, 1987.

Thompson, O. *International Cyclopedia of Music and Musicians.* New York: Dodd, Mead, 1975.

BOOKS ABOUT COMPOSERS

Ewen, David. *The World of Great Composers.* Englewood Cliffs, N.J.: Prentice-Hall, 1962.

Kavanaugh, Patrick. *The Spiritual Lives of Great Composers.* Nashville, Tenn.: Sparrow Press, 1992.

Slonimsky, Nicolas. *Baker's Biographical Dictionary of Musicians.* 8th ed. New York: G. Schirmer, 1991.

BOOKS ABOUT VARIOUS INSTRUMENTS

Arnold, C. R. *Organ Literature: A Comprehensive Survey.* Metuchen, N.J.: Scarecrow Press, 1973.

Goodman, H. A. *Instrumental Music Guide.* Provo, Utah: Brigham Young University Press, 1977.

Headington, Christopher. *The Orchestra and Its Instruments.* New York: Harper and Row, 1965.

Kendall, A. *The World of Musical Instruments.* London: Hamlyn Publications, 1972.

Klotman, R. H. *Teaching Strings.* New York: Schirmer, 1988.

Stimpson, M. *The Guitar: A Guide for Students and Teachers.* Oxford: Oxford University Press, 1988.

Walther, Tom. *Make my Music.* New York: Little, Brown and Co., 1981.

Whitener, S. *A Complete Guide to Brass.* New York: Schirmer, 1989.

Winternitz, E. *Musical Instruments of the Western World.* New York: McGraw-Hill, 1967.

BOOKS ABOUT THE PIANO

Bastien, J. *How to Teach Piano Successfully.* Park Ridge, Ill.: General Words and Music, 1977.

Fine, L. *The Piano Book: Guide to Buying a New or Used Piano.* Mass.: Brookside, 1987.

Gillespie, John. *Five Centuries of Keyboard Music*. New York: Dover Publications, 1965.

Hinson, Maurice. *Guide to the Pianist's Repertoire*. Bloomington, Ind.: Indiana University Press, 1987.

Peery, J. Craig, and Irene W. Peery, eds. *Music and Child Development*. New York: Springer-Verlag, 1987.

Schafer, R. Murray. *Creative Music Education*. New York: Schirmer Books, 1976.

Wilson, Frank. *Tone Deaf and All Thumbs? An Invitation to Music-Making for Late-Bloomers and Non Prodigies*. New York: Viking-Penguin, 1986.

BOOKS ABOUT SINGING (VOICE AND CHORAL)

Espina, N. *Repertoire for the Solo Voice*. Metuchen, N.J.: Scarecrow Press, 1977.

Henderson, L. *How to Train Singers*. West Nyack, N.Y.: Parker Publishing, 1979.

Kagen, S. *Music for the Voice*. Bloomington: Indiana University Press, 1968.

May, W., and C. Tolin. *Pronunciation Guide for Choral Literature*. Reston, Va.: Music Education National Convention, 1987.

Schmidt, J. *Basis of Singing*. New York: Schirmer, 1989.

Ulrich, H. *A Survey of Choral Music*. New York: Harcourt Brace Jovanovich, 1973.

BOOKS ABOUT DIFFERENT
MUSIC EDUCATION METHODS

Dalcroze

Vanderspar, E. *Dalcroze Handbook: Principles and Guidelines for Teaching Eurhythmics*. London, England: Roehampton Institute, 1980.

Kodaly

Choksy, Lois. *The Kodaly Method.* Englewood Cliffs, N.J.: Prentice-Hall, 1988.

Orff-Schulwerk

Keetman, Gunild. *Elementaria: First Acquaintance with Orff-Schulwerk,* trans. Margaret Murray. London: Schott and Co., Ltd., 1974.

Suzuki

Shinichi Suzuki. *The Man and the Philosophy.* Athens, Ohio: Ability Development, 1981.

Shinichi Suzuki. *Nurtured by Love: The Classic Approach to Talent Education,* trans. Waltraud Suzuki. Smithtown, N.Y.: Exposition, 1973.

MUSIC THEORY BOOKS

Dallin, Leon. *Foundations in Music Theory.* Belmont, Calif.: Wadsworth, 1967.

Evans, R. *How to Read Music.* New York: Crown, 1978.

Harder, Paul. *Basic Materials in Music Theory.* Boston: Allyn and Bacon, 1970.

Ottman, R. *Elementary Harmony.* Englewood Cliffs, N.J.: Prentice-Hall, 1970.

Piston, W. *Counterpoint.* New York: Norton 1947.

Piston, W. *Harmony.* New York: Norton, 1962.

MUSIC HISTORY BOOKS

Brockway, W. and H. Weinstock. *Men of Music.* New York: Simon and Schuster, 1958.

Grout, Donald J. *A History of Western Music* rev. ed. New York Norton, 1973.

Lang, Paul H. *Music in Western Civilization.* New York: Norton, 1941.

Palisca, Claude V. *Baroque Music.* Englewood Cliffs, N.J.: Prentice-Hall, 1968.

Westrup, J., ed. *The Master Musicians Series.* London: J. M. Dent, 1954.

MUSIC HISTORY BOOKS FOR CHILDREN

Bernstein, L. *Young People's Concerts.* New York: Simon & Schuster, 1970.

Britten, B., and Imogen Holst. *The Wonderful World of Music.* Garden City, New York: Doubleday, 1968.

Dowlely, T., and A. Orza. *The Illustrated Lives of the Great Composers Series.* Available from Music in Motion.

Thomas, Wendy. *Composer's World.* (series). New York: Viking-Penguin.

Kendall, C. *Stories of Composers for Young Musicians.* Toadwood Pub., 1982, also *More Stories of Composers.*

Ventura, P. *Great Composers.* New York: GP Putnam, 1988.

Westberg, J. *The Pantheon Story of Music for Young People.* New York: Pantheon, 1968.

BOOKS FOR KIDS

Brighton, Catherine. *Mozart—Scenes from the Childhood of the Great Composer.* New York: Doubleday, 1990.

Davol, Marguerite W. *The Heart of the Wood.* New York: Simon & Schuster, 1992.

Downing, Julie. *Mozart Tonight.* New York: Bradburg Press, 1991.

Hoffman, E.T.A. *Nutcracker.* (pictures by Maurice Sendak). New York: Crown Publishers, Inc., 1984.

Kidd, Ronald. *Second Fiddle.* New York: Lodestar Books, E.P. Dutton, 1988.

Lasker, David. *The Boy who Loved Music.* New York: Viking Press, 1979.

Nichol, Barbara. *Beethoven Lives Upstairs.* New York: Orchard Books, 1993.

Musical Instruments of the World. Facts on File Publications, Oxford, England. 1976.

Music (Instruments). Eyewitness Books, Neil Ardley, Alfred A. Knopf, NY, NY. 1989.

Schanf, Peter. *The Violin Close Up.* New York: Four Winds Press, a division of Scholastic, 1980.

Stevens, Bryna. *Handel and the Famous Sword Swallower of Halle.* New York: Philomel Books, 1990.

Van Kampen, Vlasta. *Orchestranimals.* New York: Scholastic, Inc. 1989.

Warfel, Diantha. *The Violin Case Case.* New York: E.P.Dutton,1978.

Weil, Lisl. *The Magic of Music.* New York: Holiday House, 1989.

Wolferi, the First Six Years in the Life of Wolfgang Amadeus Mozart 1756-1762. New York: Holiday House, Inc., 1991.

Index

♦ ♦ ♦